BFI Modern Classics

Rob White
Series Editor

Advancing into its second century, the cinema is now a mature art form with an established list of classics. But contemporary cinema is so subject to every shift in fashion regarding aesthetics, morals and ideas that judgments on the true worth of recent films are liable to be risky and controversial; yet they are essential if we want to know where the cinema is going and what it can achieve.

As part of the British Film Institute's commitment to the promotion and evaluation of contemporary cinema, and in conjunction with the influential BFI Film Classics series, BFI Modern Classics is a series of books devoted to individual films of recent years. Distinguished film critics, scholars and novelists explore the production and reception of their chosen films in the context of an argument about the film's quality and importance. Insightful, considered, often impassioned, these elegant, well-illustrated books will set the agenda for debates about what matters in modern cinema.

14.21 C.

The Crying Game

Jane Giles

BFI PUBLISHING

First published in 1997 by the
British Film Institute
21 Stephen Street, London W1P 2LN

The British Film Institute exists to promote
appreciation, enjoyment, protection and
development of moving image culture in and
throughout the whole of the United Kingdom.
Its activities include the National Film and
Television Archive; the National Film Theatre;
the Museum of the Moving Image;
the London Film Festival; the production and
distribution of film and video; funding and
support for regional activities; Library and
Information Services; Stills, Posters and
Designs; Research; Publishing and Education;
and the monthly *Sight and Sound* magazine.

Designed by Andrew Barron &
Collis Clements Associates

Typeset in Garamond Simoncini
by Fakenham Photosetting Ltd

Printed in Great Britain

British Library Cataloguing-in-Publication Data
A catalogue record for this book is available
from the British Library
ISBN 0-85170-556-1

Contents

Dedication

'Who knows the secrets of the human heart?'
This book is in loving memory of Daniel Guilbert (1953–1995).

Acknowledgments

My thanks to Neil Jordan and Stephen Woolley, for taking time out of their ferocious production schedules to talk about *The Crying Game*. Also to Jack Lechner, whose candid comments on the development of the film were particularly appreciated. Information or materials were generously supplied by Karen Imthurn and Sarah Evans of PolyGram Filmed Entertainment, Michiyo Yoshizaki, Liora Reich, Leslie Felperin, Sharon O'Leary, Melanie Lindsell and, especially, Phillippa Wood, without whom … Thanks also to Richard Kwietniowski. Emma Davie, Roz Kidd, Lizzie Francke and Trevor Johnston each provided insights into the mysterious ways of UK film critics. For help with stills research, thanks to Alex Fenner, Matthew Sanders at Miramax, Anne Derwent at Channel Four and Lofty at Pinewood Studios. I'm grateful to Ed Buscombe, who invited me to write this book, and to Rob White, for his help. Special thanks are due to Stuart Burleigh for astute comments and perceptive readings of early drafts.

Prologue

I first heard about *The Soldier's Wife*, as *The Crying Game* was originally known, when I was working as programme manager of the Scala, a gorgeous but dilapidated repertory cinema in London's unlovely King's Cross. It was late autumn 1991 and the Scala's owner, Stephen Woolley, told me that he needed to borrow our box-office takings to produce a new film by Neil Jordan, the Irish writer and director. Assuming this was something like normal practice, the cinema coughed up. Six months later Woolley's production company Palace Pictures had gone bankrupt, as the Scala would do the following year. The story of *The Crying Game*'s production, from script development to distribution to exhibition has been for me a salutary example, 'a tribute to the endless persuasive powers of Mr Woolley ... and the endless creative powers of Mr Jordan',[1] but one that also demonstrates William Goldman's film industry maxim: 'Nobody knows anything.'[2]

Having negotiated its UK financiers' objections to the script and casting, but unable to obtain US funds because of its triple-taboo subject-matter, *The Crying Game* finally went into production with deals yet to be closed and a budget so low that it was impossible to obtain completion insurance. Jordan described the experience as being like working in a war zone, but the financial constraints dictated a degree of concentration and channelled the collective commitment, the result of which is a leanly muscular film with a bittersweet edge and particularly focused performances.

The financial success of an independent film is intimately tied up with the media's critical response to it. The commercial conundrum of *The Crying Game* was that the central secret had to be guarded and yet the movie needed publicity in order to find its audience. In the UK the press embargo on the twist resulted in reviews that were more bemused than intriguing. Furthermore its release coincided with a renewed IRA mainland campaign, and the film failed to find critical favour for its representation of the IRA (managing to be accused of both pro- and anti-IRA propaganda). But *The Crying Game* caught the imagination of the American media, fuelled by a brilliant marketing campaign by US distributors Miramax, who (pre-emptively) billed it as 'the movie that everyone's talking about, but no one is giving away its secrets'. Nominated for six Academy Awards, the film broke the US box-office ceiling for an art-house movie. *The Crying Game*'s phenomenal success in the US once again turned around Jordan's unpredictable career, reintroducing him to Hollywood but this time with the possibility of retaining creative control over higher-budgeted films of his choice. Given that Jordan's enduring concerns are for political, sexual and racial tolerance without the disavowal of difference, this can only be a cause for optimism.

Jordan first proposed *The Soldier's Wife* in 1982, at which time he said that the story had been on his mind for several years. The basic premise was the friendship that develops between two opponents during a conflict. Jordan also wanted to contrast black and Irish experience in Britain. But he was unable to develop the project which went on to the creative backburner of his career for the next decade.

The Crying Game is the story of the redemption of its protagonist Fergus, one of Jordan's tormented heroes who must accept personal responsibility, having previously followed orders. The film itself can also be seen as a second chance taken to 'be kinder' to some of the characters from his earlier works, the themes and motifs of which are reconfigured here, confirming Jordan as a modern auteur. *The Crying Game* interrogates a triangular affair that has its roots not only in the broader history of Anglo-Irish relationships but also in the primal oedipal scenario. An exceptionally bold and seductive combination of the personal and the political, the film radically crossed over from its independent origins to ask conservative mainstream audiences to root for the love affair of an IRA terrorist and a gay transvestite. *The Crying Game* is a warning against violence and a persuasive plea for tolerance but not a 'politically correct' film as such: Jordan equates sexual difference with race, side steps the issue of homosexuality and presents its only female character as a killing machine who also has to make the tea.

The assumption that *The Crying Game* only works if you do not know that the leading lady is a man is disingenuous. When I first saw the film, I did not know exactly what I was seeing. But the second time around something clicked and I am still astonished by the way in which it grows on me. Full of premonitions and echoes, the ironic story unfolds with the dizzying logic of destiny while the pathos of the lovers' situation never diminishes. The characters feel like old friends and Stephen Rea's sad face is endlessly fascinating, still waters open to imaginative interpretation. The music sends a shiver up my spine; even the colours seem brighter. On repeated viewing every detail is in place and yet this complex, tightly realised film retains a compelling element of ineffable mystery, even when one knows its most obvious secret.

To me, a film classic is one that rewards repeated viewing, and taking another look at *The Crying Game* reveals it to be more a modern classic than a gimmicky one-shock wonder. But we no longer live in a culture of seeing movies again (and again) on the big screen. This is evidenced by the decline in the UK's characterful repertory cinemas with their idiosyncratic double bills, broken seats, resident cats and marble mosaic floors. The loss of these cinemas can be partly attributed to the advent of the video industry. (Home entertainment makes a financial nonsense of repertory, particularly during a time of recession.) Video does allow film to be studied, like turning back the pages of a book, but in an unceremonial domestic environment and on a limited visual scale. Cinema is about the magical opening out of expectations, but I wonder what we can expect to see from future film-makers whose knowledge of the classics is mediated through the small screen, with the light on?

1 Origins and Sources, Themes and Motifs

It galled his father what he played. 'What galls me,' he would say, 'is that you could be so good.' But he felt vengeful and played them incessantly and even sang the tawdry lyrics. Some day soon, he sang, I'm going to tell the Moon about the crying game. And maybe he'll explain, he sang.[3]

Neil Jordan's first book, *Night in Tunisia*, was published in 1976 when he was twenty-five years old. Looking back at this collection of short stories, one can see already many of the themes and motifs that would occupy Jordan's later work. The title story is named after a Dizzy Gillespie track, music representing the bridgeable gulf between the tenor-sax-playing father and his awkwardly rebellious son who is searching for his own voice through 'tawdry lyrics' and latterly the jazz of Charlie Parker. In the haunting 'Last Rites', an Irish labourer's fragmented final impressions of London are those of a wall, a black man and a bridge (always bridges!)[4] as he slits his wrists in a public bath. Although some of the stories are characterised by a thread of homoeroticism (such as 'Sand' and 'Seduction', in which a boy is drawn into a kiss by the tears of his friend), Jordan's work is here established as being more about the exquisitely pleasurable pain of longing than about the consummation or anticlimactic mechanics of sex.

Written just after he made *The Crying Game*, Jordan's novel *Sunrise with Sea Monster* picks up the thread of adolescent homoeroticism which had been less obvious in his work since *Night in Tunisia*, as Donal and Mouse act out the imagined erotic progress of Donal's father, Sam, and Rose, the piano teacher. But the emotional core of *Sunrise With Sea Monster* is the relationship between Sam, Rose and Donal, itself a variation on the relationship at the centre of Jordan's first novel, *The Past* (1980),[5] in which the narrator traces his mysterious parentage to discover that his young mother was caught between a much older man and his adolescent son. Nearly all of Jordan's books and films play out variations on this single most dominant theme of his work: the triangular relationship. In most cases this takes the form of a sexually naive man (the son) becoming obsessed by an older woman whose identity is a mystery to him (his mother) and who has already been claimed by another (his father). In addition to its oedipal manifestations, this relationship could be seen to represent the triangle comprising Eire, Northern Ireland and England, or the great Irish triumvirate of Church, State and Family. In *The Miracle* (1990) the aspiring writer Rose spells it out to the saxophonist, Jimmy, who has inadvertently fallen in love with his own mother:

Rose: You see, stories to do with love are mathematical. Okay, A loves B. B unfortunately does not love A but has a longing for C.
Jimmy: So what about C?
Rose: Here are various options: C can love A who loves B who loves C. Or, C can love B, but only halfheartedly. Either way the stage is set for a farce.
Jimmy: So what if A and B love C and C doesn't know what she wants?
Rose: Well then that's tragic.
Jimmy: Okay, though in fairness if A loves B and B loves A . . .
Rose: Well then there's no story.

In *Sunrise with Sea Monster,* Donal, home from the Spanish Civil War, finds himself caught up in an obligation to communicate between his German liberator and the Republican movement, while informing the police of his progress. Whimsically (romantically) designating himself 'Rhett' to Donal's 'Scarlett', the German instigates a code in which each equation is a reference to a page, a line and a word within a line. Contemplating his concurrent emotional entrapment, Donal sees the relationship between himself, his now stricken father and Rose as 'a triangular cocoon, an equation known only to ourselves that related to no known numerical system'.[6]

Jordan's literature is sensual, intimate and atmospheric, sparely written so its meanings resonate between the lines. Because so much of its power lies in sketching ineffable interior emotions, it is able to deal with relatively understated interpretations of the triangular scenario. Jordan's books have earned him considerable critical praise but little financial return; cinema, however, operates within different economies. Perhaps this is why Jordan's films (with the exception of *The Miracle*, which was a box-office disappointment) tend towards more obviously sensational variations on the triangular relationship: the pretend family of Lestat, Louis and their 'daughter' Claudia (*Interview with the Vampire*); a racist ex-convict, a 'thin black tart' and her drug-addicted lesbian lover (*Mona Lisa*); a heterosexual IRA volunteer, a black British soldier and his gay transvestite lover (*The Crying Game*).

Describing himself as 'a literary sophisticate and a cinematic innocent' (*Observer*, 31 October 1982), the twice-published Jordan set about making his first feature film, *Angel*, in 1981. Given that Ireland's literary tradition so outweighs its cinematic heritage, film – the secular and suspect medium of his childhood – represented for Jordan a liberation from 'the introspective certainties of a literary culture. An escape into chaos and colour, into narrative convulsions and juxtapositions of things that seemed impossible in books' (*Sunday Telegraph*, 31 March 1991). Just as *Night in Tunisia* set thematic precedents for his later work, so *Angel* can be seen to establish many of the cinematic ground rules

Neil Jordan at the Scala's premiere of *Angel*, London 1982

for a Neil Jordan film. The creation of a dreamlike atmosphere and the sense of a character's magical inner world take priority over adherence to classical narrative. The pleasure in inversion and subverting expectations finds its most obvious expression in Jordan's commitment to humanising 'the demons' and the film entered into an ongoing dialogue with critics about the representation of the IRA.

Angel also introduced Jordan to his long-term producer, Stephen Woolley. In the early 80s Woolley was programme manager of the Scala cinema and co-founder of fledgling distribution and production company, Palace Pictures. Falling in love with Jordan's first film at a late-night screening in Cannes, Woolley signed up *Angel* as Palace's distribution debut, opening it at the Scala in autumn 1982. *Angel* thus set a theatrical precedent for Channel 4's made-for-television movies;

a decade later the generic name 'Film On Four' would achieve international recognition following the success of *The Crying Game* in the US.

Set in the same bleak Armagh countryside as the opening sequence of *The Crying Game*, *Angel* was also Jordan's first cinematic

Angel

collaboration with the actor Stephen Rea. As the showband saxophonist Danny, Rea establishes a sensual character who is something of a fool for love. Having made out with a mute girl, Danny witnesses her murder and experiences a furious desire for vengeance muddled with responsibility and guilt.[7] Seeking a disguise after committing several revenge killings, Danny stumbles upon a remote farmhouse where he obliges a widow named Mary to give him her husband's clothes in return for his garish stage costume. Mary also cuts Danny's hair in a scene closely parallelling that in which Fergus transforms Dil into an echo of Jody. But whereas Fergus will prevent Dil from killing herself with his gun, Danny cannot save Mary from the same fate. Jordan's films individually and collectively are about redemption, and one can see in *The Crying Game* an opportunity taken to 'right' some of the tragic events in his previous stories.

Referencing Antonioni through the postcard of Monica Vitti, *Angel* is open about its origins in European cinema. Elsewhere Jordan has denied that he uses film references, though this is not to say that one cannot make connections nor that he has no appreciation of other directors' work. During press interviews Jordan has discussed the films of Nicholas Ray, Scorsese, Cocteau, Fassbinder and Fellini. But in the same breath this cultural epicurean will talk about the work of Borges, Beckett or Joyce. Cross-referencing film and literature, it seems to me that Jordan's work also echoes that of Jean Genet, both stylistically and in a shared preoccupation with themes of sexual identity, nationality, desire and betrayal. Jordan (whose mother is a painter) has equally referred to the work of artists who have influenced the look of his films: Velasquez (*Angel*), Gustav Doré and

The Miracle

Francis Bacon (*The Company of Wolves*), Poussin and Watteau (*Interview with the Vampire*).[8]

Music, too, has its place in Jordan's work. A saxophonist himself, from the very outset jazz figures in both the content and compositional form of his stories. (After all, what is black originated jazz if not sexually charged and characterised by syncopation, melodic variations and unusual tonal effects?) Both individually and across his oeuvre, Jordan's films and books send themes weaving in and out, picking up threads and finding a corner of expression in the least likely places. He is a director who has talked of 'skating through the genres' (*Daily Telegraph*, 10 December 1994), though the truth is not so much that he has systematically ticked off different types of movie (werewolf flick, Soho thriller, historical biopic ...) as that his films tend each to combine a variety of elements. The critic Simon Hattenstone has described Jordan's world as:

Messy, incoherent and fluid, one in which nothing is fully understood, nothing can be taken for granted. He continually explores but never resolves. This unpredictability is reflected not only in the themes but the work itself. He will throw in any number of disparate, even conflicting, elements – the political, the thriller, the love interest, the obscurely surreal, the bruisingly naturalistic, the supernatural, fairy tales, the mythical. The mix is so unlikely, so unbalanced, that it's hard to make comparisons.[9]

Jordan's films can be thrilling but also bewildering. Repeated viewing affords a familiarity with the internal logic of his world, while considering each film within the context of his other works allows a coherent overall project to emerge. Six movies and a decade after Jordan described himself as a 'cinematic innocent', he still claimed 'I think I haven't a clue as to how films are supposed to be made' (*Village Voice*, 6 August 1991). Jordan's belief that the complicated process of film-making exists to be bent to his imaginative purpose has resulted in the wide-ranging but idiosyncratic vision of an auteur.

2 'The Soldier's Wife', and Other Stories

Angel was applauded by critics but picketed at the Cork Film Festival by fellow directors who were furious that it had taken up the Irish Film Board's entire annual production budget (anger at the accusation was fuelled by the fact that the film's executive producer, John Boorman, was also a member of the board). Looking to the UK for his next film, Jordan first proposed *The Soldier's Wife* to Channel 4's drama department in May 1982. Jordan suggested the project in place of *The Rab*, a complex and potentially expensive historical Irish drama already at script stage, to be produced by Boorman.

Jordan initially described *The Soldier's Wife* as a film about characters rather than countries, 'a bizarre love-story, a love-story in reverse', which had been on his mind for several years. He saw it as taking up some of the themes of *Angel*, but extending these in a more subdued and personalised manner. Assuring Channel 4 that 'it has an urgency of theme and a poetry that will lead to worthwhile ends!', he acknowledged that it was difficult to give a succinct plot outline, particularly of the ending, because he did not want the thriller mechanism to take over the story. The gist of it was to contrast West Indian and Irish experience in Britain by exploring the situation of a black British soldier being held hostage by an IRA activist. Jordan's films tend to work against the more staid and verbose influences of Irish literary and theatrical traditions, but he was inspired by two previous explorations of this situation, namely Frank O'Connor's short story 'Guests Of The Nation' (1931) and Brendan Behan's 1958 play *The Hostage (An Giall)*.

O'Connor's alternately haunting and humorous story brilliantly captures the relationship that develops between a guard and his prisoner. Events are narrated in the past tense by Bonaparte, a young IRA volunteer who is one of four men guarding an odd couple of English soldiers: the taciturn but sober big man Belcher, with his 'queer smile',[10] and the loquacious little anarchist 'Awkins. Not that the men take much guarding – Bonaparte is convinced that the hostages had no thought of escaping and were quite content with their lot: 'It was and is my fixed belief you could have planted that pair in any untended spot from this to Claregalway and they'd have stayed put and flourished like a native weed.'[11] In a remote country farmhouse the group play cards, banter and argue about the existence of ''Eaven' when the command comes for the volunteers to kill the soldiers.

Bonaparte is devastated. 'Awkins is incredulous, bemused, repeatedly demanding to know, 'Weren't we chums? Weren't we? Didn't we understand him and didn't he understand us?'[12] Bonaparte recalls, 'I kept feeling my Smith and Wesson and thinking what I would do if they happened to put up a fight or ran for it, and wishing in my heart they would. I knew if only they ran I would never fire on them.'[13] 'Awkins is executed while arguing, but Bonaparte finds himself even more disconcerted by the resigned and peaceable Belcher's need to talk before he is killed and his confession that he has had no sense of home since his wife left him. Bonaparte is left saddened, a changed man: 'I was somehow very small and very lonely. And anything that ever happened to me after I never felt the same about again'.[14]

Behan's *The Hostage* is the rumbustious story of a young British soldier who has been kidnapped in protest at the imminent execution of an IRA volunteer in a Belfast jail. At the end of the first act, the blindfolded soldier arrives at an old Dublin boarding house populated by an eccentric gathering that includes volunteers (one of whom is named Feargus), whores, a homosexual navvy (Rio Rita) and his black boyfriend (Princess Grace, who at one point in the play carries a banner proclaiming 'Keep Ireland Black'). Though the IRA volunteer's execution is inevitable, the soldier's fate is uncertain thanks to the various allegiances he forms with his captors.

The soldier discovers a shared love of cricket with Monsewer, the elderly owner of the house who forgets his Republican tendencies in a song that horrifies his fellow IRA men: 'But praise God that we are white. And better still we're English – tea and toast and muffin rings, old ladies with stern faces, and the Captains and the Kings.'[15] The caretaker, Pat, almost sends the soldier out for stout, and he is nearly seduced into joining forces with Rio Rita, Princess Grace and the homosexual civil servant, Mulleady. The soldier's best chance is if the country girl with whom he has formed a romantic liaison goes to the authorities, but the informer Mulleady gets there first and the house is stormed by the police. The soldier makes a run for it but is killed in a hail of 'friendly' gunfire. He rises to sing:

The bells of hell,
Go ting-a-ling-a-ling,
For you but not for me,
Oh death where is thy sting-a-ling-a-ling?
Or grave thy victory?[16]

In his introduction to the published script of *The Crying Game*, Jordan claimed that he wanted his film to dig past the surface of friendship between hostage and captive to uncover the erotic possibility and 'sense of mutual need and identification that could have provided salvation'.[17] He found the key to this by adding a third character to the equation – Dil, who embodies the love the two men cannot express for each other. However, his original outline of 1982 was much more complicated.

Original Outline

Louis is a young volunteer with a strange and uncanny smile which expresses a warmth totally at odds with the situation in which he finds himself, guarding a black British soldier who is being tried by the IRA. The soldier seems to have accepted his fate, and tells Louis about his life with an intensity which arises from the extremity of his situation. They talk about cricket and hurling. The soldier gives Louis a photograph of his wife, a beautiful black woman, and asks him to contact her if anything happens to him, to tell her that he was thinking of her.

Something unspoken seems to pass between them. To his horror, Louis is chosen to execute the soldier. Walking out by a river the soldier asks Louis to keep talking as a bag is slipped over his head. Unable to shoot, Louis is pistol-whipped by one of the other IRA men and falls to his knees beside the soldier. A shot rings out through the landscape.

Louis goes to London where he gets work on a construction site. He tries to forget the past, but everything he meets serves as a reminder. Louis plays hurling at weekends and confesses to an Irish priest. He studies the photograph of the soldier's wife. One afternoon Louis goes to see a cricket match between Britain and the West Indies. That evening he telephones the soldier's wife but cannot bring himself to speak. Instead he composes a courteous and elaborate letter describing a fictitious chance encounter with her husband and expressing sympathy with her bereavement. To Louis' surprise he receives a reply, and a brief correspondence leads to a meeting. Falling in love, Louis seems to believe the stories that he invents for the soldier's wife. The couple compare their backgrounds and experiences of both being strangers in British society. They rarely mention the soldier, although his presence remains between them.

Louis' idyll is shattered by the return of people from his past and he hides out at the apartment of his new love. That night she whispers the name of her dead husband: Lewis, to which Louis responds. The soldier's wife probes him and realises the depth of his deceptions from the conflicting replies, but Louis leaves her before revealing the full truth. He wanders the streets, sleeping rough. One night in a bar he meets a black girl named Caroline who reminds him of the soldier's wife, in a rough kind of way. Louis asks to go home with Caroline, who eventually agrees. She tells Louis that he is just a boy, but when he opens her blouse he discovers that she is actually a man. This is the climax of all distortions. Caroline now reminds Louis of the soldier. The couple sleep chastely beside one another and in the morning Caroline tells Louis about her imaginary past. His self-deceptions are matched by her gentle unrealities and their fantasies unravel themselves over the next few days as Notting Hill prepares for the Carnival. Caroline seems to understand Louis and helps him to come to terms with his past by being both the soldier's wife by day and the soldier himself by night.

Jordan promised that the different threads of the story would come together during the Carnival weekend.

Though he usually finished a script within four or five weeks, Jordan failed to develop this storyline following the publication of Bernard MacLaverty's novel *Cal* (1983) in which a reluctant IRA recruit falls in love with the widow of an RUC policeman for whose death he feels responsible.[18] The similarities between *Cal* and the basic plot of *The Soldier's Wife* were strong enough for Jordan to feel that his idea had been usurped.[19] So the script of *The Soldier's Wife* was put on hold for nearly a decade, during which time Jordan's enduring concerns were played out in five other movies and a short book.

Jordan's second film was *The Company of Wolves* (1984), a Gothic version of the 'Little Red Riding Hood' fairy tale adapted from a story by Angela Carter and apparently worlds away from the comparative realism of *Angel*. Jordan had been encouraged to explore this fantastic subject matter by Woolley, who had recently distributed Sam Raimi's art-house horror movie, *The Evil Dead* (1982). Combining the mythology of werewolves with a sensual exploration of adolescent sexuality, Jordan's film has fear and desire deliciously mixed up as the beast inside men meets its female match. Made up of stories within stories within dreams, its key theme of transformation echoes that of Jordan's febrile novella, *The Dream of a Beast*.[20] Stephen Rea plays a handsome lupine traveller who disappears on his wedding night when he steps out to answer a 'call of nature'. Anticipating Jody's fairground plight in *The Crying Game*, the traveller's distraught bride is convinced that the wolves 'came and took him when he was making water – when a man is at his most defenceless!'.

Inspired by Nat King Cole's rendition of the eponymous song by Jay Livingston and Ray Evans, Jordan's next film, *Mona Lisa* (1986), is the story of a man who always gets things wrong about women. A dark film with a generous heart, it combines elements of different genres to create a movie that is at the same time comedy and thriller, romantic love story and sleazy flick. Bob Hoskins plays George, a newly released ex-convict – half saint, half idiot – who heads like a homing pigeon back to a place where he is no longer welcome. George, Danny (*Angel*) and Fergus (*The Crying Game*) are all men haunted by their past mistakes. Trapped, but still trying within probably unjustly hopeless situations, they belong nowhere and are never at home. George is given a job as driver to Simone (Cathy Tyson), an elegant prostitute or 'tall thin black tart', as he calls her. She calls herself 'the girl that men run home from'. The initial animosity between this odd couple starts to turn when Simone transforms George into a well-dressed man. He becomes infatuated and intrigued by her apparently selfless mission to rescue her friend Cathy,

a juvenile hooker long lost on the mean streets of King's Cross. Blinded by love, George jokes that Simone is a nun in disguise. He searches the Soho underworld[21] and tries to win her by tracking down Cathy, only to realise that she is the one whom Simone loves.

An early cut of *Mona Lisa* showed the sexual consummation of George and Simone's relationship. This scene was eventually removed as it curtailed the plot, which is driven by George's longing. In the climax of the film, Simone is cornered in a hotel bedroom by the three men who threaten the future of her relationship with Cathy. Simone shoots dead the sinister duo of her abusive former pimp and her boss, but she

The odd couple: Cathy Tyson and Bob Hoskins in *Mona Lisa*

is also capable of killing George because she cannot love him. When George realises this, he will not take the rap for Simone in the way that Fergus can for Dil, who loves him.

Following the critical and commercial success of *Mona Lisa*, Jordan went to Hollywood. Slated as a 'complete turkey' (*Time Out*, 7 December 1983), the disastrous *High Spirits* (1988) represented a low point in the working relationship between Jordan and Woolley. Accustomed to tight budgets[22] and to filming nothing but what he could see in his head, Jordan's $16 million movie became a sprawling mess as he shot extra footage, including costly animatronics that barely appeared in the final cut. Jordan explained that *High Spirits* was taken out of his hands in post production: 'I thought I was making a sort of *Whiskey Galore* but the American producers had a different view. They wanted a raucous teenage comedy' (*Evening Standard*, 5 April 1991).

Jordan was unable to blame screenwriter David Mamet for the relative failure of *We're No Angels* (1989), a comedy which few found funny. Nevertheless, he felt that he had betrayed himself by working from someone else's script on what was essentially a studio's star vehicle, and had allowed his destiny to be taken out of his own hands.

At this point Jordan returned to Europe to pursue more personal projects over which he could exercise greater control. Relating to his own 'scribbling background', his personal favourite among his films, *The Miracle*, is set around the nun-swept seaside town of Bray, its fairground prefiguring the opening scenes of *The Crying Game*. Recalling the triangular familial relationships and adolescent anguish that pervaded Jordan's earlier literature, *The Miracle* has a clear echo of 'Night In Tunisia' when Jimmy is berated by his showband saxophonist father: 'That's what galls me – that you could be so good.' Rapturously received at the Berlin Film Festival, *The Miracle* was hailed critically as Jordan's return to form after Hollywood. It was at this moment – and in this place – that the long-gestated story of *The Soldier's Wife* finally clicked.

3 'The Crying Game'

Full of optimism from the festival response to *The Miracle*, Jordan
went out to a Berlin club with Woolley. It was here that he came up with
the twist to the soldier's story: what if the soldier's wife turns out to be
a man? Suddenly everything fell into place – as Woolley later said,
'I thought this was fantastic, the best thing I could have imagined.
It would confront everything about Irish men by sending [Fergus] on
a journey that is far removed from his own macho world. All the rules
would break down.'[23] During the decade following Jordan's first
proposal of *The Soldier's Wife*, Pat O'Connor (who had directed 'Night
In Tunisia' as a television drama in 1983) made his feature debut with
an adaptation of *Cal* (1984). Although the basic idea of a reluctant

What if?

volunteer falling for the widow of his victim had remained, Jordan felt liberated by the fact that the film of *Cal* had prioritised politics and realism rather than the personal odyssey of its protagonist. Jordan would later describe how he finally found a way of writing the script of *The Soldier's Wife*:

When I started to write this script I just thought, Look, I don't care what you 'can' or 'cannot do'. Can you start the opening of your film basically like a one-act play, with two actors sitting in one place? Of course you can. Can you suddenly shift and make the audience think they're going to see a story that's about the hard-bitten facts of politics and then suddenly turn it into a psychological thriller? Or a love story? Of course you can. You can do whatever you want.[24]

Fired up by the idea of the twist, Woolley hammered Jordan to produce a script in time to seek financing at Cannes in May 1991. Having spent ten years thinking about *The Soldier's Wife*, Jordan wrote the script in just ten days. The final story goes like this:

Synopsis

A black British soldier named Jody is lured away from an Armagh fairground by an Irish woman, Jude, and then suddenly kidnapped by the IRA. Held hostage in a glasshouse[25] while the IRA try to negotiate with the RUC for an exchange of prisoners, Jody befriends one of his captors, Fergus. Jody shows Fergus a photograph of his beautiful wife, Dil, and asks him to look out for her should anything happen to him. Fergus is instructed by his boss Maguire to execute Jody, but finds himself unable to shoot his escaping prisoner in the back. Jody is hit by a British tank as troops arrive to storm the glasshouse.

Fergus escapes to London where he takes a job as a labourer on a site overlooking a cricket pitch. Remembering his promise to Jody, he discovers Dil working as a hairdresser at Millies salon in Spitalfields. She cuts his hair, and guesses that Fergus is Scottish. Fergus follows Dil to

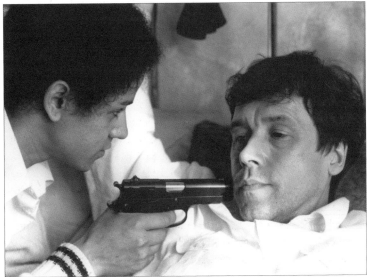

(Top) Premonitions
(Bottom) Echoes

the Metro, a club presided over by Col, the genial bartender. Fergus tells Dil that his name is Jimmy. He saves her from a troublesome boyfriend, Dave. Gently haunted by Jody's memory, the couple begin a tenuous romance, but when they eventually make love Fergus is horrified to abruptly discover that Dil is in fact a male transvestite.

Fergus lashes out at Dil and runs away. At first she refuses his apologies, but Dil later visits Fergus at work and their relationship is tentatively (although not sexually) resumed. Jude and Maguire catch up with Fergus to inform him that in his absence he has been court-martialled by the IRA and sentenced to the suicide mission of assassinating a British judge. They tighten the screws on him by threatening to involve Dil. Fergus tries to protect Dil from Jude and Maguire by cutting her hair and disguising her in Jody's old cricketing whites. But, drunk and distraught, Dil refuses to stay hidden. Fergus admits to her that he knew Jody. As Fergus sleeps, Dil ties him up and holds him at gun point causing him to miss his appointment with death. Instead, Maguire is killed during the assassination. Jude catches up with Fergus but is shot dead by Dil who then turns the gun on herself. Fergus saves Dil by telling her to go to the Metro while he prepares to take the rap for the murder of Jude. Why? Because it is in his nature. Dil stands by her man, visiting Fergus in prison with only two thousand three hundred and thirty-five days left to go.

To Woolley's astonishment and disappointment, American investors such as Sony and Miramax did not take to the project as strongly as he had expected. It was not just that *The Miracle* had quietly misfired, despite its success in Berlin; the problem was the taboo-breaking subject matter. According to Jordan, 'one executive said it was more than his career was worth even to be associated with it because it dealt with race, sexuality, political violence. One of those things would be bad enough, but having all three was enough to send them running for the door' (*Daily Telegraph*, 19 February 1993). The film was eventually financed without American money but also without the contingent editorial demands of American financiers.

The first setback in finding European financing for *The Soldier's Wife* came when the cash-flush new French investment company CiBy 2000 claimed to love the script but passed on the project perhaps predicting that its founder Francis Bouygues would not sanction the film's central revelation.[26] Around £1 million of the budget eventually came from Eurotrustees – a consortium of UK, Spanish, German, French and Italian film distributors (Palace Pictures being the UK member) – which had been set up the previous year to address the problem of American hegemony in European cinema. *The Crying Game* was to be the only production funded by the consortium since agreement across the group was too difficult to achieve. A further £350,000 was put in by Michiyo Yoshizaki's Japanese distribution company, Nippon Development & Finance. British Screen Finance had

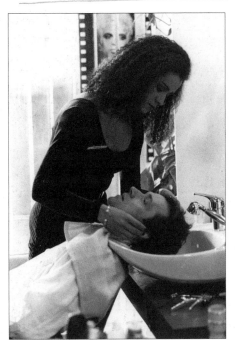

invested in several of Palace's productions, but having lost money and found that the scheduled repayments of loans were not forthcoming, this source of finance was in jeopardy. However, the script found special favour with the company's new chief executive, Simon Perry, and British Screen contributed £500,000.

The balance of the £2.3 million budget came from Channel 4, whose well-established relationship with Jordan, Woolley and the film's

Premonitions

executive producer, Nik Powell, was inherited by the new head of drama David Aukin and his assistant commissioning editor, Jack Lechner. But though Jordan had by now streamlined the narrative of his original outline, the development of the script reached stalemate. Channel 4 felt that Jordan's strategy of presenting Dil on her own terms as a woman before revealing her to be a transvestite would seem like a freakish trick and backfire, whereas audiences should be capable of accepting a transvestite as a sympathetic character from the outset. The commissioning editors were also convinced that once Dil had revealed herself to be male the rest of the film would be an anti-climax. Furthermore, Fergus' behaviour after the revelation was seen to beg credibility. There seemed no way around this problem – the elements to which Channel 4 objected were built into the very fabric of the

Echoes

screenplay; the story simply didn't work for them. Despite being accused of 'fiddling around with the script'[27] Aukin and Lechner were determined that *The Soldier's Wife* would not go into production until what they saw as the film's flaws were fully addressed.[28]

The casting also caused problems. Jordan had written the role of Jody for Forest Whitaker, who had played Charlie Parker in Clint Eastwood's 1988 biopic *Bird*. Jordan was convinced that few others had the charisma to pull off the film's 'Stockholm Syndrome in reverse'[29] while masked. Woolley had to persuade Channel 4 that the casting of the American actor in the role of an East London squaddie would pay for itself in terms of international sales and American box-office success. But black members of the UK actors' union Equity objected and attempted to get the Department of Employment to refuse Whitaker a work permit. The black press backed the campaign, asking 'What about our boys? Brian Bovell or Gary McDonald would both have been excellent for this part' (*The Voice*, 6 October 1992). Palace agreed to pay Equity a small fee in recompense for the casting of an American actor, but not before Woolley had tetchily responded, 'We are making a film with a reasonably large budget by UK standards. The only way to do this is to cast an internationally recognisable actor in the role ... I understand what they are saying, but if Palace didn't make successful pictures, we'd go bankrupt, and that would harm the employment of black actors far more than giving the role to Forest Whitaker' (*Independent*, 1 November 1991).

Some critics remained sceptical, describing Whitaker's accent as 'wandering all the way from Tottenham to Timbuktu' (*Sunday Telegraph*, 1 November 1992). Whitaker was also accused of looking 'more like a sumo wrestler than a squaddie' (*The Voice*, 6 October 1992). While it is true that the actor's bulk makes him seem an unlikely cricketer and an even less likely soldier, his girth marks him out and crucially suggests that Jody is different from the rest. Like that of Belcher in O'Connor's 'Guests of The Nation', Whitaker's presence has a literal as well as a spiritual solidity. His weight also makes Jody's final flight seem all the more miraculous.

Channel 4 was even more concerned about the casting of English actress, Miranda Richardson, as the IRA volunteer Jude. The commissioning editors found this decision inexplicable given the number of 'genuine' Irish actresses available and were concerned that Richardson would present a threat to the film's authenticity. Woolley rebuffed this charge with a volley of examples of successful casting against nationality, and the choice of Richardson was eventually vindicated. Channel 4's Jack Lechner gladly admits that he was wrong, describing the actress as 'a true protean who can become anything and anyone she needs to be'.[30] Richardson proved that she could even *cough* with a Belfast accent. The critic Philip French praised her performance as 'sexuality transformed into lethal politics' (*Observer*, 1 November 1992), although detractors included Anne Billson, who found it 'one-

Different from the rest: Forest Whitaker as Jody

note' (*Sunday Telegraph*, 1 November 1992). In the end, Richardson's credibility aside, the casting of a British actress as an IRA member works ironically and subtextually, suggesting to us that this is not a person to be trusted.

The screen persona of Stephen Rea (Fergus), by contrast, is that of someone to be relied upon, though the press were keen to point out his political connections (a Belfast-born Protestant turned Catholic, he is married to Dolours Price, one of the two Price sisters jailed in 1973 for their parts in an IRA bomb attack on the Old Bailey). The role of Fergus was written for Rea, who sees the characters Jordan creates for him as fictional versions of the film-maker himself: gentle, abstracted, tortured and confused, innocents lost in a hard world ('but he's about as innocent as Kissinger', *Guardian*, 2 January 1995). In turn, Jordan has said that he uses Rea – who reminds him of Jean-Paul Belmondo or Jean Gabin – repeatedly for his unadorned style of performance which conveys the character's inner being ('he's got a face that you can project every thought into . . . He's like a lens for the whole story', *The Orange*

Two-faced: Miranda Richardson as Jude

County Register, 24 November 1992). Although Jordan is not necessarily 'an actor's director', in both *Angel* and *The Crying Game* the collaboration between himself and Rea generated the screen magic of an inspired partnership (comparable to that of Martin Scorsese and Robert De Niro, for instance). Woolley describes the chemistry between them:

Neil inhabits an area of the intellect which is to do with dreams. In a way there's a charm to that, but like a lot of Irish charm it can be overpowering if it's not tempered. The world that Stephen Rea as an actor and theatre producer has been involved in is more modern and pragmatic. If you can combine a realist with a fantasist then that's where the chemistry comes. Individually it may be difficult, but together they give you confidence.[31]

'A lens for the whole story': Stephen Rea as Fergus

The press heralded Rea as 'magnetic, dissonant' (*Sunday Times*, 1 November 1992) and it was thought that 'his gentle, ironic charisma creeps up on you, and makes his particular form of heroism all the more touching' (*Newsweek*, 30 November 1992). Philip French observed that Rea's Fergus 'exudes troubled probity' (*Observer*, 1 November 1992) while Jack Lechner compares the actor's presence to that of Humphrey Bogart, saying 'Stephen projects intelligence on screen ... he's simultaneously tough and vulnerable; there's a sadness in his eyes which softens even his hardest moments,'[32]

Among others, it was Jordan's friend Stanley Kubrick who warned him that the key role of Dil was probably uncastable, and for a time this prognosis seemed correct. Tipped off by Derek Jarman, Palace's casting agent Susie Figgis eventually spotted Jaye Davidson. Well known on the club scene, Davidson had worked as a fabric buyer for dress designers David and Elizabeth Emmanuel and was once sacked from a hairdressing job for being rude, but had absolutely no acting aspirations. Davidson's laconic, subtle persona grew on the film-makers through the lengthy auditioning process and many try-outs. Davidson says he finally took the role only to pay for a pair of exquisite, hand-made black leather riding boots. Jordan had to 'trick' Davidson into acting by turning a

costume fitting into a rehearsal into a take before the reluctant star had time to think about what was going on (*Premiere*, US, December 1992).

The risk of casting the inexperienced Davidson in the role of Dil paid off magnificently with the additional benefit that as a first-time actor his sex remained unknown to more of the public. Apart from the comment in the *Financial Times* that Davidson 'drifts

Almost impossibly right: reluctant star Jaye Davidson

through his role's androgyne mysteries in a bewildered monotone' (29 October 1992), most critics concurred that Davidson was 'almost impossibly right' (*Variety*), quite literally a revelation for his unclichéd performance, delicacy and vulnerability.

But these future accolades were far away. Uncompromising on cast and script, having slashed shooting schedules, shaved the budget and relying on partially deferred salaries, Woolley had to secure the film's finance with no weapons left other than an emotional evocation of the joint history of Palace Pictures and Channel 4 as they grew up together in the 80s, sharing a mixture of hits and flops. Since no other television company would dare finance a film with this subject matter, *The Soldier's Wife* would not be made without Channel 4's participation. Woolley bombarded the company's Charlotte Street offices with hourly phone calls, begged, and threatened to set himself on fire in the foyer. As Palace's former PR assistant Angie Errigo later commented, 'to Nik and Steve, it was always a matter of life and death'.[33]

The intended start date of July 1991 came and went and, with it, Jordan's vision of the story unfolding beneath bright blue summer skies. Channel 4 and Palace were deadlocked between the 'take it or leave it' attitude of the latter and the former's determination not to proceed with a script about which they had reservations. After the failure of *The Miracle* Jordan was more inclined to return to Hollywood than work on personal projects and had convinced himself that 'whatever you say about the American way of making films, at least they're not negative' (*Independent*, 23 October 1992). He would have walked away from *The Soldier's Wife* had Woolley not broken the cycle of development hell by taking Jordan and Lechner out of the bureaucratic fund-raising arena to work together on the script for a few days in Ireland. Here, Jordan proved more amenable, and as a result of some final script changes, *The Soldier's Wife* finally got the go-ahead in late September 1991.

Palace's problems were not yet over. Unable to agree a deal structure for the film, Channel 4's finance department abruptly passed on the project and, once again, Woolley and Powell had to resort to bombarding the channel with hourly phone calls until the financial hiccup was sorted out in mid-October. But the production company still had to meet an early November start date to secure the above- and below-the-line deferrals which would make the budget work. Two other Palace Pictures films were also currently in production (*Waterland* and *Dust Devil*) and the company was in the throes of an aggressive audit. Foundering financially, Palace was unable to provide the necessary cash flow for the *The Soldier's Wife*, which had started shooting with production finance deals yet to be closed and with a budget so low that it was impossible to secure the completion bond required by banks and other investors as insurance against the film going way over budget. The film was thrown into a crisis after just three days of shooting when salaries, fees and other bills became due. Most of the cast and crew had turned down more lucrative offers to stay with *The Soldier's Wife* and their patience was nearing its end. When Jordan himself threatened to walk off the set, Woolley was reduced to using his personal credit cards and raiding the meagre box-office takings of his cinema.

By the end of the second week of shooting, the American director of photography, Frederick Elmes,[34] had left the film because of working differences with Jordan, who was covering the ground of his gruelling schedule with a furious intensity 'fuelled by the realisation that if he did not pull it off, *The Soldier's Wife* would possibly be his last film for a long time'.[35] Although peppered with minor disasters, the discipline of the pared-down shoot in Laytown, County Armagh, primed the cast and crew for the move to outer-London's Shepperton Studios. By this point the collective commitment had been effectively channelled and Woolley was to say that everyone on the set felt that something really special was being created. Jordan was to declare that he would be unlikely to work in Britain again, in part because of the severe funding restraints which made shooting *The Crying Game* 'about as much fun as making a film in Zagreb' (*Daily Telegraph*, 18 February 1993).

Having miraculously managed to meet the pre-Christmas shooting completion date, the first rough cut of the film came in at the end of

January 1992 at two hours and thirty-five minutes. Although both Channel 4 and Palace Pictures were pleased with the results, there was an overriding problem with the ending. According to Jack Lechner,[36] Channel 4 had been dissatisfied with the ambiguous original ending of Jordan's script in which Dil visited Fergus in prison and gave him a copy of Freud's *Interpretation of Dreams*. So Jordan wrote a new ending in which Fergus escapes over the rooftops following Jude's murder. The hapless Dave arrives looking for Dil, only to be arrested. Under police interrogation Dil presents a convincing front of innocence and bewilderment. Cut to a white Christmas, one year later. A lonelier Dil finds a customer waiting in Millies salon – it is Fergus, with a new identity. They banter about a cash windfall and an escape to Barbados, and the closing line references the famous punchline of *Some Like It Hot*: 'Nobody's perfect'.

According to Woolley, Jordan was willing to live with this second ending before he started making the movie, 'but when we saw what we were getting in terms of performances and how the story was working he realised that he'd made a mistake. By the time that Neil came to shoot the ending of the film, his heart wasn't in it'.[37] Although Nik Powell maintains that the interrogation scenes convincingly drew together the threads of the film's personal and political storylines, he also described the ending as 'the cutest thing you've ever seen'.[38] The relatively whimsical and happy-go-lucky mood was too glib and lighthearted for so complex a film and everyone agreed that a bittersweet rather than a sugary conclusion was needed. Jordan quickly wrote a third ending. Basically a wittier, sharper version of his original idea, the scenes of an incarcerated Fergus telling Dil Jody's story of the frog and the scorpion were shot at an extra cost of £45,000.

By April 1992 the film had also acquired a new title: *The Crying Game*. Stanley Kubrick had advised Jordan that films with religious or military titles were off-putting to audiences and having witnessed the commercial failure of *The Miracle*, Jordan was inclined to agree. The new title was taken from Dil's theme tune, a dignified and heavy hearted ballad heard in three different versions throughout the film, the 'tawdry lyrics' of which are familiar from Jordan's short story 'Night In Tunisia'. Dil listens to the original version of the song, which was a hit for British teen idol Dave Berry in 1964. She also lip-synchs to 'The Crying Game' (sung by Kate Robbins) onstage at the Metro. Heard over the end credits, the final version is a seductively playful but knowing cover by Boy George, produced by Neil Tennant and Chris Lowe of the Pet Shop Boys. Boy George's involvement was the deciding factor for Woolley in titling the film after what could be a hit single. Boy George insisted on checking the movie before participating, explaining that he 'wanted to make sure it wasn't some hideous, war-mongering, homophobic nightmare' (*Rolling Stone*, 4 March 1993).

The songs used diegetically or over the credits of *The Crying Game* tend to function ironically and they contrast with the film's actual score. Jordan commissioned Anne Dudley to orchestrate background music inspired by the work of Estonian classical composer Arvo Pärt (particularly his piece in memory of Benjamin Britten). Simultaneously sad and hopeful, the score circles and grows to convey a sense of destiny unfolding. Other sequences invoke a sense of threat through an ominous undercurrent of humourless military-type music.

The film was finished just in time to be considered for the all-important Cannes festival. Co-producer Elizabeth Karlsen (Stephen Woolley's wife) went to the festival office in Paris clutching their new-born baby daughter Edythe in one arm and *The Crying Game* in the other. Having previously admired a rough cut of the film, the festival director Gilles Jacob now told Karlsen that he found *The Crying Game* 'a little bit too Anglo-Saxon', feeling that its flaws lay in the difference of the first act from the rest of the movie. The seven-strong jury turned down the film – twice – by four votes to three. Declining to overrule the jury's decision, Jacob said, 'Democracy was the reason for *The Crying Game* not being selected for Cannes'.[39]

4 United Kingdom and Ireland

In April 1992 Palace Pictures was officially declared bankrupt.[40] Palace was co-founded in 1982 when former Virgin partner Nik Powell joined forces with one-time ticket-tearer Stephen Woolley to revitalise The Other Cinema, an old-school art-house theatre in the West End. This cash-haemorrhaging operation was reborn as the Scala, an idiosyncratically marketed American-style repertory cinema whose eclectic, daily-changing programme incorporated everything from cult movies to the classics. But Palace was primarily formed as a video distributor to cash in on the burgeoning home entertainment market, before moving into film distribution and then production. The company became infamous as the brats of the British film industry, unpopular

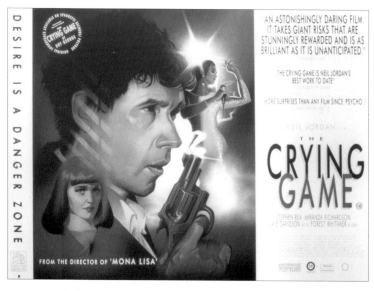

among rivals for its aggressively passionate strategies. Palace's adage was that there is no such thing as too much hype, and rather than sweeping mistakes under the carpet, critical flops were routinely turned into social

Mayfair's UK campaign: 'lacklustre'

phenomena. But for every flop there was a hit, such as *Mona Lisa*, Palace's follow-up to the lavishly flawed *Absolute Beginners*.

Towards the late 80s Palace over-diversified, moving into pop promos, television, recording studios and too many loss-making businesses while their latest productions flopped and the company suffered a dearth of distribution hits. Like so many companies set up in the 80s, Palace was built on credit and crashed when the recession-stung banks pulled back on their lending. Palace left around £18 million of debt and a lot of ill will which was still raw when *The Crying Game* was released in the UK on 30 October 1992, distributed by another company, Mayfair, as part of a pre-insolvency deal.

The film's release coincided with a renewed thrust in the IRA's campaign on the mainland, which perhaps made the press wary of *The Crying Game* but certainly raised the stakes in the ongoing discussion about the cinematic representation of the IRA. Hugo Davenport commented that 'the recent plague of bombs in London will, no doubt, make it harder than usual for British cinemagoers to accept the notion of an IRA man with a conscience turned too delicate for the dirty work of terrorism' (*Daily Telegraph*, 29 October 1992). Tom Paulin later slammed Jordan as a southern Irish film-maker who knows nothing about Northern Ireland, saying '*The Crying Game* is a shockingly awful film. It's so sentimental, just propaganda for the IRA' (*Guardian*, 2 January 1995). The film was also condemned for glorifying the IRA by Ulster Unionists, with the MP William Ross comparing the fiction to that of films about the Great Train Robbers, saying 'the reality is that they create a false impression' (*Observer*, 10 January 1993).

Stephen Rea argued that the conflict is only extended by the promotion of the popular myth that anyone who represents the nationalist movement in Northern Ireland must be a mindless madman. He stated that:

The IRA has done terrible things, but what's important about the way the film approaches that reality is that they've become people they didn't want to be. That doesn't mean the cause is wrong ... Fergus has a choice to make, to go their way and expunge his own feelings, for this hostage he's face-to-face with, and kill him, or recognise that what he originally thought of as just another British soldier is a human being.[41]

Jordan was mystified by suggestions that the film was sympathetic to the IRA, saying:

Jordan's view

I did not set out to make any moral judgments on these people, not on the IRA or the British Army. I aimed to portray them as people stuck in situations where they have to do unacceptable things. I think the IRA do unacceptable things and wish they would stop, but I don't think it helps to censor consideration of political violence.[42]

During the production of *Angel*, Jordan had had to call in the Special Branch for protection following a sinister and silent nocturnal visit to his home by persons unnamed. At this time he said, 'Irish politics are quite complex and I felt the place to make a comment on them wasn't in a feature film' (*NME*, 31 November 1982). *Angel*'s political thread is narratively underplayed, though the film's sense of division and threat is virtually tangible. Interviewing Jordan at the time of the simultaneous publication of *Sunrise With Sea Monster* and the UK release of *Interview With The Vampire*, Simon Hattenstone described him as finding politics a puzzle and as someone in whom political contradictions abound, striking 'a common chord amongst millions of similarly confused people' (*Guardian*, 2 January 1995). Jordan is a republican, 'in the old-fashioned sense' as he told the *Daily Telegraph* (10 December 1994), but his politics reflect his preoccupation with the difficulties of moral choices and his ambivalence is in contrast with what he has called the 'horribly coherent view' of the IRA (*ibid.*).

In addition to invoking wrath by having refused to demonise the IRA in his characterisation of Fergus, Jordan was also criticised by some Republicans for following the standard line of humanising only the terrorist who wants out, and for the film's villainous portrayal of Jude. Jordan told the *Irish Independent* (30 October 1992) that he got the idea for this part of the story from a newspaper account of IRA activists who preyed on soldiers in bars and enticed them back to their apartments for sex, saying 'this practice was so distasteful that it was eventually stopped by the IRA themselves'. So Jordan was accused of both pro-IRA and anti-IRA propaganda, echoing the exchange between the English Soldier and the Irish Officer in Behan's *The Hostage*:

Soldier: Brendan Behan, he's too anti-British.
Officer: Too anti-Irish, you mean. Bejasus, wait till we get him back home. We'll give him what-for for making fun of the Movement.[43]

Among Irish film critics, *The Crying Game* was considered Jordan's best work to date. The *Irish Times*' influential Michael Dwyer characterised it as 'a tantalising and unconventional contemporary thriller which turns unexpectedly romantic and is laced with dry, ironic humour ... a heady concoction that is richly inventive and brilliantly sustained' (30 October 1992). The *Irish Independent*'s Philip Molloy wrote 'if any Neil Jordan film works, this is it. It has depth and pace and humanity ... *The Crying Game* is that unusual thing: a complex adult movie of ideas that makes you care deeply about its characters' (30 October 1992).

The best UK reviews came in the Sunday papers, whose critics are traditionally thought to be more reflective than those of the daily press, and some of whom certainly have more column inches in which to write around their subjects. The most considered and enthusiastic response was from the much-respected Philip French, who declared, 'this is storytelling of a major order, beautifully paced, strongly atmospheric, morally challenging, authoritatively acted' (*Observer*, 1 November 1992).

Although *Variety* (2 November 1992) tallied ten UK critics in favour of the film, with only three mixed reviews and none completely against it, looking in detail at the overall response reveals a rather less rosy picture. The UK critics were bemused by PR company pleas not to reveal the twist and commented on this in their reviews, making it sound as though they were dutifully exposing a con man's cheap gimmick. Nigel Andrews declared the film unreviewable without disclosing the 'body-blow surprise' and so advised potential viewers not to read his review (*Financial Times*, 29 October 1992). The sense was very much of the critics refusing to join in the game. The most hostile review came in the conservative tabloid, the *Daily Mail* (30 October 1992). Describing the film as 'faintly distasteful', with its 'preposterous storyline about hard-to-credit people', the reviewer proclaimed it 'a failure', though he also acknowledged his subjectivity and half-heartedly reminded readers that they could always make up their own minds by seeing it for themselves.

More characteristic were mixed reviews which offered praise peppered with reservations and the self-fulfilling doubt that the film would find its audience. The two-part structure was criticised as broken-backed, coming under fire from those who liked the first half but not the second (or vice versa). The multitude of themes was blamed for making the film 'too many-faceted for its own artistic life' (*Financial Times*, 29 October 1992), losing the viewer 'in the crossfire between mystery thriller and message movie, between Antonioni enigma and meanstreets melodrama' (*ibid.*). The twist was seen as 'spurious' (*Sunday Telegraph*, 1 November 1992), if not off-putting: 'Will [Jordan's] trap door of surprise become a pitfall of disgust?', asked the *Mail On Sunday* (1 November 1992). *Time Out*'s Geoff Andrew accused Jordan of heavy-handed tactics resulting in a film that lurched 'from one contrived moment of shock to another' (28 October 1992) while the *Guardian*'s Derek Malcolm reckoned that the film could have been more intriguing had it further explored the relationship between Fergus and Dil. *Today*'s conclusion that Jordan's film (which 'alternately shows him at his maverick, atmospheric best and his dippy, off-beam worst') is 'an intriguing effort worth seeing on a slow night' (30 October 1992) is not a million miles away from the *Independent*'s bottom line that 'even if *The Crying Game* is only almost terrific, it deserves to be celebrated' (30 October 1992).

The mixed reviews would not have been so much of a problem were it not for the lack of other media coverage. Editorial and feature articles can be crucial to a film's success, being more cost-effective and credible to potential audiences than advertising. But Jordan described trying to get magazine coverage for the film as like 'rowing through glue' and *The Crying Game* was heralded by little more than a dull article on the problems of filming on location in London. On the eve of the film's release, Woolley berated the newspaper arts editors and television media producers (rather than cinema critics) for having declined to cover the film because they considered its content to be 'too strong meat'. To Woolley, ignoring the film was ignoring the horrendous reality of the Troubles, and he astutely predicted that the ultimate irony would be achieved if *The Crying Game* was a flop in Britain and a hit around the world (*Guardian*, 30 October 1992).

Jordan maintained a pragmatic position on the question of critics, saying that 'there are very few people who are truly incisive. First you're overpraised, as I have been, and then you're overblamed, as I have been, but your films exist somewhere in between' (*What's On*, 28 October 1992). But Woolley believed that critics were 'sharpening their knives and going for a pound of Palace flesh'.[44] Palace had certainly antagonised the UK film establishment (some parts of which gloated over its bankruptcy) and Woolley had openly heaped scorn on the mostly aging, white male critics who set themselves up as intellectual and cultural arbiters while being astonishingly ignorant of the workings of the industry whose end results they so often dismissed. In comparison to their American counterparts, Woolley characterised UK critics as 'untalented, underpaid, frustrated myopic cretins' (*Guardian*, 20 February 1993).

Woolley also felt that Mayfair failed to book the film to its best advantage and slammed the UK's disdain and apathy towards British cinema, saying '*The Crying Game* was released here with a sense of predestined failure' (*Independent*, 26 March 1993). *Variety* described the film's marketing campaign as 'lacklustre' (*ibid.*) and it certainly opened without the tub-thumping fanfare and publicity hype characteristic of

Woolley's previous productions. Nonetheless, *The Crying Game* generated solid if not spectacular box-office figures in London. In an exit poll carried out during the film's opening, 35 per cent described the film as 'excellent' and 36 per cent as 'very good', with 55 per cent agreeing that they would definitely recommend it to others. Forty-seven per cent had been influenced to see the film by reviews (63 per cent gave the fact that the film was by Neil Jordan as their reason for attending). Without editorial coverage or unconditional rave reviews, the film's best chance would be through positive word-of-mouth generated around a sustained 'platform' run, but the opportunity for this was blown by opening the film too wide in the capital and too soon in the regions. By Christmas 1992 *The Crying Game* had made just £300,000 in the UK, although it later proved to have legs by sustaining a longer run in a single venue, buoyed – ironically – by editorial coverage of its six Academy Award nominations and its phenomenal popularity in the US.

5 United States

North American rights to *The Crying Game* were bought for between $1 and 1.5 million by Miramax, the independent 'mini major' production and distribution company that had co-produced some of Palace's previous pictures and shared its 'brattish' reputation. Having passed on the original script, Miramax chief Bob Weinstein now declared *The Crying Game* to be 'one of the greatest movies I've ever seen'.[45]

The American buzz on *The Crying Game* started when it showed at the Telluride, Toronto and New York film festivals in autumn 1992. Audiences were impressed by (rather than suspicious of) Woolley's passionate introductions to the film in which he implored them not to reveal the plot to those who had yet to see the movie. In an influential review, *Variety*'s Todd McCarthy described *The Crying Game* as 'an astonishingly good and daring film that richly develops several intertwined thematic lines, [taking] risks that are stunningly rewarded' (14 September 1992). This positive response was consolidated by the all-important *New York Times* critic Vincent Canby (26 September 1992). The tone had been set for the American critical response.

Whereas UK reviewers had picked at *The Crying Game*, the US critics unreservedly declared it to be the film of the year and tackled it in the manner of a starving gourmet approaching a delicious feast. The structural twist was compared to Hitchcock's films *Psycho* and *Vertigo*. Shakespeare's comedies were cited. The film's ironic black humour was repeatedly praised. The *New Yorker*'s Terrence Rafferty quoted Yeats and described the film as a fable about how a warrior becomes a true hero and the revolutionary process by which a soldier reinvents himself as a poet and lover.[46] Whereas the British press (and public) were probably put off by the spectre of terrorism, the US has 45 million Irish-Americans and no IRA on the doorstep. The *Financial Times'* Christopher Dunkley has further argued that 'Americans confuse America's fight for independence with the activities of Irish terrorists so that the IRA becomes a right-on organisation on their side of the

Atlantic' (1 November 1994). *The Crying Game* was also critically revered as an exploration of the blurred nature of love, trust and compassion and the unpredictability of human emotion. The taboos of interracial relationships, 'perverse' sex and terrorism became the film's strange points of attraction. Critics celebrated rather than reviled *The Crying Game* for tackling so many different issues, revelling in the fact that it was four types of movie in one.

UK critics had been made grumpy by the press embargo on Dil's sex, but their counterparts in the US gleefully competed to see who could write the longest article that gave the least away: 'At the request of the film-makers, reviewers have taken a blood oath not to reveal the twists of this astonishing, darkly amusing, dizzyingly romantic thriller ... Quick – go see it for yourself!' (*Cosmopolitan*, January 1993). *USA*

Miramax's
US campaign:
a brilliant hook

Today warned that 'anyone who divulges the second plot twist of this handsome, terrifically acted movie deserves to share the fate of *Game*'s most loathsome character' (25 November 1992).

Above all, it seemed that the way in which the film confounded expectations was the main cause for celebration and much of the critical rhetoric was concerned with the achievement of the impossible. *The Orange County Register*'s review (24 November 1992) encapsulated the overall American critical response to the film:

The Crying Game is one of the year's best movies. And the very qualities that make it so engaging and surprising would have kept it from being produced by any American studio. This movie refuses to play by conventional rules; it's fresh, funny, tragic and gloriously unpredictable . . . The narrative takes daring and unexpected turns that leave your head spinning and cause you to re-evaluate everything you've seen – Jordan starts detonating genre expectations . . . Just when you think you know where The Crying Game is going, it delights you by going someplace else . . . This is a movie about overturning preconceptions – about people and about movies.

Opening the film in late November 1992, Miramax's lavish advertising campaign centred on the 'conspiracy of silence', confidently (pre-emptively) declaring this 'the movie that everyone's talking about, but no one is giving away its secrets'.[47] The hook worked brilliantly and intrigued audiences flocked to play the game, whether thanks to a real hunger for something different or because consumers tend to respond slavishly to the latest craze (be it the hula-hoop, *Twin Peaks* or Hard Candy nail polish). Press articles appeared about the rush to see the film ('Queuing for *The Crying Game*', *Time*, 1 March 1993) and about the marketing campaign itself, debating whether the 'Big Secret' was just a big gimmick. Wave upon self-generating wave of publicity maximised the film's life at the box office.

The film's release coincided with Bill Clinton's election success, and Woolley reckoned that *l'air du temps* was one of optimism, a time when serious issues could be combined with entertainment (*Time Magazine*, 25 January 1993). In early 1993 *The Crying Game* received renewed editorial coverage as a reference point in the debate about the proposed end to the ban on gays in the US military and it generated yet more press soon afterwards when it was nominated for six Academy Awards. The Oscars may not be a measure of art, good taste or common sense, but they do reflect the commercial mood of Hollywood with unerring accuracy. The *New York Times'* Frank Rich noted an anti-war or anti-machismo theme shared by contenders *The Crying Game*, *Unforgiven*, *A Few Good Men* and *Scent of a Woman* ('Clintonian Cinema', 21 March 1993), all of which describe a hero who is a pacifist (except in self-defence), misty-eyed and in touch with his feminine side. Rich points out the similarity of this model to Clinton himself, who escaped being drafted to Vietnam and who has made empathy an artform. The villains of the piece, on the other hand, tend to be either uniformed lunatics or full of George Bush-like bellicose splutter.

A decade before the Academy's recognition of *The Crying Game*, *Tootsie* (Sydney Pollack, 1982) had been nominated in as many categories. The gender confusion that this comedy vehicle for Dustin Hoffman flirts with lies at the heart of Jordan's film. But while Hollywood acknowledged a new mood, it had yet to go as far as considering an openly celebratory gay movie. As the independent film-maker James Toback commented, 'Hollywood has taken a step toward the cliff edge, but it's in no danger of jumping off' (*Sunday Times*, 28 March 1993).

During the period between the first release of *The Crying Game* and the Academy Awards, Miramax strategically increased the number of release prints from six to 239 to more than 1,000, indicating that the film was accessible to a mainstream audience in addition to its art-house appeal. The press was amused that the Academy had effectively blown the film's carefully guarded secret by nominating Jaye Davidson as Best Supporting Actor. An Academy spokesman commented, 'it's very

unfortunate we had to give away the secret, but the members felt
Mr Davidson's performance was worthy of recognition. It would not
have been honest to have nominated him in the best supporting actress
category, despite the fact that he makes a wonderful girl' (*Daily
Telegraph*, 18 February 1993). The film's other nominations were for
Best Film, Best Director, Best Actor (Stephen Rea), Best Film Editing
(Kant Pan)[48] and Best Original Screenplay. Although *The Crying Game*
lost out respectively to *Unforgiven*, Clint Eastwood (*Unforgiven*),
Al Pacino (*Scent of a Woman*) and – again – *Unforgiven*, Neil Jordan won
the Academy Award for his screenplay. In his acceptance speech,
Jordan said:

It was a difficult script to write. People said to me it was about characters
that were unappealing and would be unappealing to audiences at large.
But I think that the way audiences have responded to this film has taught
me that they have it in their hearts to embrace any range of characters and
any range of points of view.

The financial success of *The Crying Game* in the US was astonishing. It
became 1993's most profitable film based on the gap between negative
cost and domestic gross, and was the only independent production to
figure in the top fifteen titles. Reckoning a budget of $5 million and a
box-office take of $59,348,005, the film's ratio of 11.9 was nearly double
that of the second most profitable title, *Jurassic Park* (*Screen International*,
14–20 January 1994). *The Crying Game* would far exceed the supposed
$25 million box office ceiling for art house movies, grossing around $68
million in the States. Although little of the profits filtered back to the
UK (where the final box office take was around £2 million), the film's
financial success abroad only increased the acrimony of Palace Pictures'
creditors.

Soon after the completion of *The Crying Game* Jordan wrote his
first novel in nearly a decade, *Sunrise with Sea Monster*, because, he said,
'it looked like the game was up for me in films' (*Evening Standard*,

13 January 1995). But the critical and commercial success of *The Crying Game* in the US was responsible for turning around once again the director's unpredictable career.[49] Two years earlier, Jordan had commented ruefully that 'I don't particularly want to do what the studios want me to. The things that I want to do which could cost a lot of money, I don't think are bankable.'[50] Now, however, Hollywood was offering him considerable budgets to make the films of his choice on his own terms.

Jordan's next project was a lavish $60 million adaptation of Anne Rice's best-selling novel *Interview with the Vampire* for Warner Bros. (1994). Within Jordan's oeuvre, this fantastical, febrile fairy tale can most obviously be compared to *The Company of Wolves*, though it also features more than a few echoes of *The Crying Game*. As Fergus was a reluctant terrorist, so Louis the vampire is loathe to kill. The film shrugs off the more obvious genre trappings of Bram Stoker's novel *Dracula* (dismissed by Louis as 'the demented fictions of an Irishman!') in favour of dramatising the triangular emotional entrapment of the vampires. Desperate to become a woman, Claudia tries to destroy her childish identity by shearing off her golden locks, though unlike Dil's hair her curls immediately reappear. The struggle between Lestat and Louis shivers on the verge of a physical affair and the film is something of a paean to homoerotic interest, particularly as Jordan cast the hottest male sex symbols in Hollywood at the time: Tom Cruise, Brad Pitt and Antonio Banderas.[51]

Jordan's intention was to alternate higher budgeted studio movies with more personal projects. His next film was one that had been on his mind for as long as that of *The Soldier's Wife*: the story of Michael Collins.[52]

6 Taking Another Look at the Twist

Channel 4 broadcast *The Crying Game* during the Northern Ireland ceasefire in November 1994.[53] Although the cinema attendance figures of around 500,000 had been disappointing, the film had fared well on video in the UK with 25,000 units sold for rental and c. 40,000 on sell-thru. The nature of the twist had become relatively common knowledge thanks to media coverage of the Academy Awards, yet the television critics sustained the 'conspiracy of silence', even when sniping that the film was 'overrated' (*Independent*, 29 October 1994) and 'not as good as they thought in the US' (*Financial Times*, 1 November 1994). Most reviews were (more or less) in favour of *The Crying Game*, but the film was not reconsidered assuming the prior knowledge that the soldier's wife is a man.

Rewatching *The Crying Game* affords the viewer familiarity with the perhaps initially bewildering inner logic of Jordan's world. It enables one to get beyond the shock value of the twist and see how this complex film is both genuinely original and deeply old-fashioned. *The Crying Game* is a modern love story set against a contemporary war, yet the film's sense of Fergus' destiny and emphasis on gallantry seem like something out of time. Fergus is himself caught between past and future, between Jude (the devil he knows) and the deep blue sea of Dil. These two characters are continually compared or contrasted, but the film is ultimately more concerned with masculinity than femininity.

Contrary to the film's American press campaign, the narrative success of *The Crying Game* does not rely on its audience believing from the outset that Jaye Davidson is a woman. This film is about the redemption of Fergus, from whose point of view the story is told. Fergus assumes that Dil is a woman until the moment he sees she is not. Jaye Davidson's Dil, therefore, had to be convincing or the audience would not believe that Fergus could mistake a he for a she. But Dil is not *so* convincing that the viewer reels in disbelief at the film's sleight of hand, and on a second viewing one can see that Jordan has 'played fairly' by giving plenty of hints and double entendres among a whole shoal of red herrings. Jude accuses Fergus of being a walking cliché, but as a transvestite hairdresser isn't Dil the (heterosexual) cliché of homosexuality? Stephen Woolley later said, 'We gave away so many gay clues, it always shocks me that anyone doesn't get it. Particularly Londoners. If we'd really wanted to con the audience into thinking that Dil was a woman we would have had a much quieter performance, with no singing in clubs or throwing goldfish out of the window.[54] The question, then, is not 'how did they do that?', but 'why didn't I realise?'

Jody's fairground frolics with Jude are the equivalent of Dil's self-destructive dalliance with Dave the Essex man: both kick sand in the eyes of the viewer, who may as well be watching the noisy courtship of any badly dressed heterosexual couple. But in the rarefied atmosphere of the glasshouse where the buzzing of a fly sounds as loud as a helicopter, every word is loaded: a matter of life or death. Jody has fixed on Fergus, after having determined from listening, silently hooded, that he is the most sympathetic of his captors (the one who offers tea, despite the fact that he previously kicked his hostage in the head). Through apparently guileless personal prattle about cricket and his childhood, Jody not only forges a connection with his captor but gets himself right under the Irishman's skin. On second viewing, Jody's strategy to win over Fergus seems not only charming, but disarmingly flirtatious:

Jody: You're the handsome one with the killer smile and the baby face.
Fergus: Am I?
Jody: Yeah. And the brown eyes.
[Fergus pushes the last crumbs of the sandwich toward Jody's mouth.]
Jody: You're the handsome one.
[Jody eats the last bits.]
Jody: Thank you, handsome.
Fergus: My pleasure.[55]

Pissed off at having to help Jody urinate, Fergus eventually finds his hostage's good humour infectious. Having politely replied 'my pleasure' twice before, Fergus now quips that 'the pleasure was all mine!', their mutual laughter confirming the bond between the two men. Jody's language is sprinkled with expressions of humour ('Only joking'; 'You know the funny thing?'; 'This is a farce'), but he does not waste his breath trying to make the intractable Maguire laugh. Jody draws a distinction between Fergus' kind nature and that of his people ('you're all tough undeluded motherfuckers'). He illustrates his point with the fable of the frog and the scorpion, which proposes that there are two types of people in the world: those who give generously and those who take, viciously.[56] Through both subtext and narrative, the film proves Jody's thesis by refusing to draw a line between English and Irish, men

Divisions blurred

and women, hetero and homo; each division is blurred – in the casting of actors against nationality, by making the leading lady a man and in talking about homoeroticism rather than homosexuality.

'She your wife?' asks Fergus, having taken the photograph of Dil from the wallet inside Jody's pocket (this is done slowly, with an ominous build up of music as if the wallet could be booby-trapped – which it is, in a manner of speaking). 'She wouldn't suit you', warns Jody playfully. But when Jude whacks Jody in the teeth with her gun he rails against women, offering up some oblique clues to the identity of his 'special friend': 'Women are trouble . . . Some kinds of women . . . Dil wasn't trouble . . . [I] love her. Whatever she is.' By asking his captor to tell his wife that he was thinking of her, Jody will, in effect, both deliver Fergus from Jude and protect Dil from Dave. In this sense, the music underscoring Jody's recognition of his impending death is simultaneously sad and hopeful.

The film's music spirals inexorably towards the morning of Jody's execution, becoming increasingly urgent as Fergus walks the soldier through the golden autumnal forest. Sizing up the situation, Jody uses the emotional ground he has gained to risk breaking into a surprisingly agile run, taking a last chance that (like the character of Bonaparte in O'Connor's 'Guests of the Nation') Fergus will not shoot him in the back. The two men seem almost like children playing a game of chase in the woods. Then suddenly, shockingly (and with appalling irony), Jody is hit by a British tank, heralding a climactic attack on the glasshouse which is engulfed by flames the colour of the forest.

Like Jody's frog, Fergus must now go across the water ('to lose myself awhile', as he says). No longer a soldier but just another Irish émigré labourer with cement dust in his hair, Fergus could be the anonymous, suicidal subject of Jordan's story 'Last Rites'. Then the cricket pitch opposite the site where he works reminds Fergus of his promise to Jody and he dons his best suit to seek out Dil at Millies salon. Sensuously cutting Fergus' hair, Dil thinks that her new customer is Scottish. Fergus – or 'Jimmy', as Dil will come to know him – concurs, fuelling the loss of what was once most important to him: his national identity.

Fergus follows Dil to the Metro, a fantastical haven where he is soon welcomed as a regular by the bartender, Col. Col treats Dil like a lady and solicitously mediates between the couple. Dil is always seen from Fergus' point of view, but rarely in a straightforward way: Fergus follows Dil voyeuristically, glimpsing her through blinds, veils and mirrors, courting her with a series of looks:

Dil: See that, Col?
Col: See what, Dil?
Dil: He gave me a look.
[. . .]
Dil: There, he did it again.
Col: Saw that one.
Dil: What would you call it?
Col: Now, that *was* a look.[57]

The night after he meets Dil, Fergus dreams of Jody. Although entranced by this exotic woman who bewitches him with her mime to 'The Crying Game', it is Fergus' enduring preoccupation with Jody that prevents him from seeing Dil clearly. Even when Dil is giving him a

blowjob, Fergus' eyes are fixed on a photograph of Jody, which transforms itself into a climactically fast-bowling version of his dream. Jody continues to exist between them as Fergus obsessively questions Dil, 'What would he think? . . . Did he come here too? . . . Did he dance

Fergus as Jim, just another Irish labourer

with you? … Did he ever tell you you were beautiful? … Would he have minded?'

As Dil and Fergus smooch to the war widows' song, 'The White Cliffs of Dover', she probes – but not too deeply – whether or not he is having her on. That night as the couple prepare to make love, Fergus' anticipation builds with the film's music. Dil's robe drops to reveal a flat chest, tattooed upper arms and a penis. The film falls silent, accentuating the inevitable gasps, giggles and groans of the audience. The unveiling of Dil's sex is completely unambiguous, although some viewers apparently persist in believing that Davidson is a woman.[58] Marjorie Garber describes the spectators' 'disavowal' of Davidson's sex in *Vice Versa: Bisexuality and the Eroticism of Everyday Life*: 'Their problem was the same as Fergus's: They had come to desire that which, once they "knew" what it was, they "knew" they didn't desire. Or did they?'[59]

The momentary nature of the visual revelation caused other problems. Former head of Paramount Pictures, Brandon Tartikoff, told Stephen Woolley that he didn't understand the ending of *The Crying Game*. It transpired that Tartikoff had been watching the film on video in his office when he was distracted just before Dil's revelation.[60] A version of this story made its way into an episode of the television show *Larry Sanders*, in which a viewer remained under the impression that Dil was a beautiful chick.

On the other hand, Cynthia Heimel was probably only half-joking when she wrote, 'Some of my friends told me that the popularity of *The Crying Game* is due to the primal resonance of its subject matter – we never really know the person we love, we can love people who are fatally flawed, etc., etc. But I personally think that the appearance of a bigger-than-life penis right in our faces is what got everyone excited' (*Independent On Sunday*, 28 March 1993). Long before Dil's full-frontal revelation, the film draws attention to, but does not show, the penis.[61] In the UK and US this image is hidden from the audience's curious and scrutinising gaze by systems of film classification that barely bother about a woman's body but coyly hide the signifier of masculinity. In Japan the image of pubic hair is prohibited by the self-regulating film industry, posing a problem for NDF, the distributors of *The Crying Game* who had invested in the production.[62] To cut the film would have made a nonsense of the story, but the usual solution of obscuring the offending pubes with a hovering globe of white light was aesthetically unacceptable to Jordan. Michiyo Yoshizaki explained that a compromise was reached by darkening Dil's pubic area so that the image was barely visible.

Instead of clearly showing the male sex, mainstream films of most countries connote phallocracy via a system of hard objects (most often the gun), amalgams of power, fear and desire that defend, misrepresent and stand for the vulnerable penis. While in other ways *The Crying Game* does not disavow difference, it radically breaks the taboo of male nudity to propose that genitals are mere details, of no more importance than a piece of meat.

Fergus' dream of Jody

Fergus crumples in the face of heterosexual man's darkest fear: his desire for another man. He reasserts himself by lashing out at Dil and then vomits in a crisis of (self)-disgust. That night Fergus dreams of Jody laughing at him, having won the game as Dil's revelation forces a reappraisal of all that has gone before. 'What were you doing in the bar if you didn't know?' she yells at him, and when Fergus returns to the Metro he sees that it is indeed a place for gay transvestites.[63] After the revelation, Dil herself remains the same, but the film changes tone to hit its comic stride. Dressed up to the nines and carrying a picnic basket, Dil's arrival at the building site where Fergus works is heralded by the traditional chorus of wolf whistles. Fergus' objectionable boss Deveroux asks if Dil is his tart:

Fergus: She's not a tart.
Deveroux: No, of course not, she's a lady.
Fergus: She's not that either.[64]

Dil arrives at the
building site

Dil pours the bemused Fergus a nice cuppa, in an ironic parallel to the tea-drinking scenes of Jody's captivity. Fergus muses, 'You're something else, Dil, you know that?', to which she responds, 'Must be something in the genes.' Ba-boom. When Dil is insulted again by Deveroux, Fergus gallantly defends her honour with a threat of violence ('Did you ever pick your teeth up with broken fingers?'), and 'unwisely' agrees to another date. That evening Fergus asks Dil if everyone knew except for him: Jody, Dave, the girls in Millies ... Fergus' situation is archetypal; he is the butt of a folk devil that has been explored in many other contexts, from elegant literature to homophobic and misogynistic jokes.

For instance, in Balzac's novella *Sarrasine* (1830) the eponymous unworldly sculptor falls in love with the Roman opera singer, La Zambinella, only to learn what everyone else already knows: that she is actually a man. Furious and humiliated, Sarrasine confronts the former object of his desire:

... *To love, to be loved!* are henceforth meaningless words for me, as they are for you. I shall forever think of this imaginary woman when I see a real woman ... I shall always have the memory of a celestial harpy who thrusts its talons into all my manly feelings, and who will stamp all other women with a seal of imperfection! Monster! You who can give life to nothing. For me, you have wiped women from the earth.[65]

Brandishing his sword at La Zambinella, Sarrasine is dispatched by three henchmen sent by the singer's mentor. La Zambinella grows old grotesquely, a 'human wreckage' infecting fashionable parties with his deathly chill.

Dil's sex is the ultimate challenge to Fergus, but perhaps his redemption will also be her salvation? Knowing that she is not a woman, Fergus nevertheless kisses Dil good night. At this moment there is a possibility that the couple could live happily ever after, but the film abruptly turns another corner, reintroducing the threat of Fergus' past in the form of Jude.

Jordan was accused of misogyny for his portrayal of Jude, the heartless IRA volunteer who sexually ensnares Jody, grabs Fergus by the balls and calls Dil a 'sick bitch'. Other critics relished the characterisation; the *Morning Star*'s Nadia Joseph praised Richardson's representation of Jude as 'refreshing to see a woman portrayed as they often are in reality – totally focused on her mission in life' (31 October 1992). Jude is first seen in the fairground wearing a working-class good-time-gal's uniform of snow-washed denim mini skirt and clutching a teddy bear that is as sugar pink as Jody is black. Having carried out her role in the abduction, Jude arrives back at the IRA's hideout in motorcycle gear and thereafter wears baggy, neutral clothes. In London she appears out of the shadows, having transformed herself into a sleek urban *femme fatale* with a 'tougher look' of tight designer armour, a

Good-time gal

helmet-like bob and a gun in her handbag. 'Suits you', says Fergus to
Jude, echoing Jody. Jude dresses for the assassination in front of a three-
piece mirror, recalling *The Lady from Shanghai* (Orson Welles, 1948). The
military tattoo that is her signature tune sounds a death knell. The sexual
jealousy of a spurned woman fuels Jude's commitment to duty, and she
turns the screws on Fergus by threatening Dil, the 'wee black chick'.

Jude stalks Dil in a dark parody of Fergus' journey of infatuation:
getting her hair trimmed at Millies, showing up at 'their' Indian
restaurant and lying in wait at the Metro. Here Fergus is excruciatingly
caught between his two 'girlfriends', who face each other like a couple of
cats. Dil takes a swipe at Jude's age. Jude jibes that Dil is a little heavy
on the powder. When Dil flounces out of the Metro, Col tells Fergus to
follow her, but Jude and Maguire get to him first. Having twice denied

Soldier

that Dil is a girl, Fergus now tells his abductors that she is indeed, 'just a girl' (but admits that she is 'definitely unusual' between the sheets).

Despite its irony and dark humour, *The Crying Game* is unusual in that it does not use a man in a dress as a vehicle for conventional comedy (or as an emblem of psychotic derangement). In films such as *Some Like It Hot*, *Tootsie*, *Mrs Doubtfire* or *Nuns on the Run*, for instance, the audience is introduced to the male character(s) before they are obliged to disguise themselves as women. The joke is that of watching what we know is a bloke in a frock find himself in heterosexual heaven, surrounded by beautiful women whom he can look at but not touch. Dil is no 'wolf in sheep's clothing', nor is she a dame or self-referential drag queen. Dil is truly 'something else': a gay male transvestite, at home in golden sequins.

Femme fatale

To protect Dil from Jude and Maguire, Fergus disguises her as a man. Persuading Dil to let him cut her hair, Fergus agrees, in a roundabout way, that he likes her better that way. By forcing the shorn, weeping Dil into cricketing whites, Fergus turns her into a true travesty, a pale shadow rather than a viable reconstruction of Jody. But at this point in the script, it becomes evident that Fergus loves Dil:

Fergus: Good-bye Dil.
Dil: Jimmy?
Fergus: What?
Dil: Don't go like that.
[She looks at him, standing up. Something incredibly attractive about her.]
Dil: Can't help what I am.
Fergus: Can't help what I am.
[He walks slowly toward her. He kisses her, on the lips.]
[We see the photograph with the soldier's smiling face. Fergus looks from it to her.][66]

In the same way that critics withholding the Big Secret resorted to 'an archaic vocabulary of euphemism and insinuation' ('A Crying Shame', *New Republic*, 1 March 1993), so in some ways homosexuality is for *The Crying Game* the plotline that dare not speak its name. In his role as mediator, Col cannot find the words to tell Fergus the truth about Dil:

Col: You came to see her, didn't you?
[Fergus shrugs. He takes out a cigarette. A guy in leather to his left smiles at him.]
Col: Something I should tell you. She's –
Fergus: She's what?
[The barman looks up toward the stage]
Col: She's on.[67]

This 'unnaming' is less an effect of the censorship (or self-censorship) that can make films such as *Cat on a Hot Tin Roof* confusing, but rather a result of the fact that Jordan's interest lies more in the homoerotic possibilities of the triangular relationship than in homosexual consummation. Fergus' discovery is not that he is 'really' homosexual, but that one adapts to the demands of love in a loveless world.

Cathy Tyson was present at the auditions for *The Crying Game* as a reference point for the film-makers, who found themselves floundering in a sea of female impersonators. Davidson's Dil would eventually bear an uncanny resemblance to Tyson's Simone, although Jordan claims that this wasn't deliberate or an in-joke. Having ruled out the male actors whose large features could not pass for those of a woman, Woolley later commented that Tyson seemed so much more masculine than the female impersonators who were unable to tone down their performances. Davidson's triumph was his apparently artless performance, of which Jordan observed: 'When you get someone who's never acted before, what you see is their inner dignity. Their spirit is what comes through, because they've got no technique – all they've got is themselves' (*New York Times*, 17 December 1992).

Unsurprised by his failure to win the Academy Award for Best Supporting Actor, Jaye Davidson commented, 'It would have been an insult to all the real actors if I'd won.' However, this is not to say that Davidson was simply playing himself in the film. The actor is not a transvestite and does not intentionally try to look like a woman, although is constantly mistaken for one: 'I went to the Ritz where men have got to wear suits and ties. I'm sitting there in a whole suit and they were still calling me "Madame". I just thought, Whatever' (*Interview*, November 1994). But Davidson was not shocked to be asked to act in drag, saying 'I knew they wouldn't want me to play a gunslinging truck driver' (*Rolling Stone*, 1 April 1993). Excited speculation surrounded the question of what Davidson would wear to the Academy Award ceremony in March 1993, as if this would have been a frock rather than 'a black Rifat Ozbek coat over cream jodhpurs and black thigh-high boots with his long black hair in a bun' (*Daily Mail*, 31 March 1993). Rewatching *The Crying Game*, one recognises in Davidson's performance the nuances of the London gay scene. A public declaration of his homosexuality seemed hardly an issue for Davidson; seated close to Jodie Foster and Jane Fonda for the interminable Academy Award ceremony, he told the press that he was interested in neither: 'I just want Richard Gere. Preferably naked. On the floor in front of me' (*Daily Telegraph*, 31 March 1993).

Woolley said that 'Dil would love old 40s and 50s female icons such as Bette Davis. His own emotions are mixed up and his actions are those of a fantasy creation rather than the behaviour of a modern woman.'[68] Dil tends to refer to the construct that is herself in the third person: 'You're not having me on, are you? 'Cause Dil can't stand that . . .

And she does get very upset.'[69] In doing so, Dil also echoes the speech patterns of Jody (who told Fergus, 'Jody's always right'): both characters rarely use the word 'I'. When the drunken Dil faints, complaining of 'a blood condition', she is making herself as vulnerable as possible in a cry for help that she cannot articulate. At this point the film is not necessarily pathologising race (by referencing sickle cell anaemia, for instance) or

Simone, *Mona Lisa*

homosexuality (through invoking AIDS). Like a character in one of Ophuls' or Sirk's 'woman's pictures', Dil is suffering from 'ennui' rather than a real disease: she is dying of love.

Jordan says that his interest in West Indian characters sprang from working with black navvies on building sites when he first came to London, during which time he developed a romanticised view of the Caribbean. But *The Crying Game* is focused on Fergus, and the characters of Jody and Dil can offer up only partial truths about the human beings they represent. For instance, the racism experienced by Jody in Northern Ireland ('the only place in the world they call you nigger to your face')[70] serves mainly to prefigure that encountered by Fergus in London. In a letter to the *New York Times*, Jordan's use of black characters was condemned as 'just more of the same exploitation that dates back to Stepin Fetchit' (7 March 1993) for repeating and failing to interrogate a reactionary equation between sexual and racial difference. *The Crying Game* certainly has a precedent in a minor clutch of British films which use black actors to play characters whose sex is ambiguous.

In the anarchic *Eat the Rich* (Peter Richardson, 1987), the transsexual actor Lanah Pellay plays Alex, the leader of a people's

Dil

revolution. Black, with an effeminate voice, long braided hair, make-up and earrings, but also besuited and flat chested, Alex's sex is unspecified but never a narrative issue in this political satire.[71] By contrast, the question of Jo's gender drives the entire narrative of *Girl/Boy* (Bob Kellet, 1971). Based on David Percival's play *Girlfriend*, this bizarre film concerns the Masons, a middle-aged couple welcoming home their son Laurie (who has been undergoing psychiatric treatment) and his new girlfriend Jo. Although Jo was played by a white man in *Girlfriend*, the black actor Peter Straker was cast for the role in the film adaptation. Puzzled but relieved by Laurie's sudden show of interest in the opposite sex, the Masons are then perplexed by Jo's ambiguous appearance and try unsuccessfully to determine whether she is male or female.[72] Like *The Crying Game*, *Girl/Boy* concludes that one should simply love; it

Lanah Pellay in
Eat the Rich

does not matter which sex.

In the tradition of withholding information about the actor's sex to fuel the illusion of the character,[73] *Girl/Boy* credits Jo as being played by 'Straker'. Names as ambiguous signifiers of identity are a running theme of *The Crying Game*. When Fergus first asks Jody his name, the soldier replies 'Fuck you'. Forest Whitaker's character is obviously a man, but the name Jody is as androgynous as that of Jude. (In the original script of *The Soldier's Wife* Miranda Richardson's character was called June, an ironically sunny name replaced by that of a traitor.) The name 'Dil' is also not gender-specific. Perhaps it is short for Dil-emma, though in retrospect Jordan suggested that the name may have associations with the word 'dildo', an ersatz penis. Ironically, Dave calls Dil 'cunt' (or 'scrag-eyed fucking dumb dyke carrot cunt', to be precise). His identity shattered, Fergus – Everyman or 'Mr Nobody' – is the only character in the film with many different names: Soldier, Paddy, Jimmy, James, Pat, Fergie, Hennessy, Mick, plus Dil's endearments of Hon, Darling, My Sweet, Light of My Life ('Don't call me that!', he uselessly tells her). When Dil first hears Jude say 'Jimmy's' real name, she asks, 'What's Fergus?'

    Entertainment Week reckoned that only ten per cent of American audiences guessed the true sex of Jaye Davidson's character in advance (12 February 1993). Among those in the know, the writer and drag actor Charles Busch declared, 'I couldn't believe that that was the big surprise everybody was talking about. It's no surprise to *me* that a girl has a dick. So I kept waiting for the big twist. I thought Miranda Richardson was going to reveal that she had a dick, too. I mean, *there's* a surprise for you' (*Rolling Stone*, 1 April 1993). Jude may not

have a 'dick', but she is a phallic, pistol-packing woman who wears her own kind of drag. Like Dil, Jude visits Fergus at work, but rather than bringing him tea and sympathy she delivers a gun for his suicide mission and tells him to 'forget about the girl'. But Fergus is unable to leave Dil,

'Straker' in *Girl/Boy*

who is drunk, drugged up and in male drag; he reveals to her that he knew Jody, even killed him in a manner of speaking. Dil points an unsteady finger at Fergus, quietly intoning, 'Bang . . . .'

As Fergus sleeps, Dil ties him to her bed with black silk stockings (remember the lyrics of the Mungo Jerry track 'Baby Jump' heard in the fairground as Jody is abducted?) and holds him at gun point. Dil plays her theme tune, 'The Crying Game', as she sadly puts the words that she wants to hear into Fergus' mouth: 'Love you, Dil . . . I'd do anything for you, Dil.' Meanwhile, Maguire is shot dead during the assassination of the judge. The hellbent Jude bursts into Dil's flat with her gun at the ready but Dil emerges from her veiled bed and shoots first, in Jordan's words 'like a child, playing with a toy' .[74] Accusing Jude of having trapped Jody ('You used those tits and that ass to get him, didn't you'), Dil shoots her in the throat before she can reply. Demanding to know what Jude wore when she got Jody, Dil turns the gun on Fergus, but her hand shakes: Jody will not let her kill him. Sitting at the mirror which is also her shrine to Jody, Dil silently places the barrel of the gun between her lips.

Throughout the film Fergus has repeatedly apologised to Dil, but in the end he is given the chance truly to atone, to prove that he is noble and brave. Fergus redeems himself by saving Dil from suicide and taking the rap for the murder of Jude. Framed back-to-back with a photograph of Jody ('You should have stayed at home'), Fergus prepares to take the place of his former hostage, imprisoned in a 'glasshouse'.

When Dil strides majestically into the dreary prison, resplendent in a leather mini coat and big earrings, the film's cycle is completed as Fergus explains why he is doing time for Dil: 'As the man said, it's in my nature', telling his own version of Jody's fable. In Jordan's troubled fairy tale the frog has willingly kissed the prince, which is a step in the right direction, perhaps even a giant leap for mankind. The film *does* believe in its message ('No greater love, as the man says'), but seeing Fergus isolated in his cage within the cold, grey prison causes the viewer to consider at what cost.

Films tend to avoid overwhelmingly negative or unhappy endings which send the audience away depressed. While both 'Guests of the Nation' and *The Hostage* end tragically, Jordan's elaboration of the same premise is wryly optimistic. Evoking the film's opening shot in reverse, the camera pulls back out of the prison, tracking across rows of other women visiting their men. The pleasure of seeing Fergus and Dil reunited is underscored by a lyrical summation that always makes the audience smile: 'Sometimes it's hard to be a woman ...' (the opening line of Tammy Wynette's 'Stand By Your Man' sung by Lyle Lovett). Perhaps the last scene of *The Crying Game* does not fully resolve or explain all that has gone before it, but having illustrated the irony of the lovers' situation, Jordan also suggests that there may be hope for our divisions yet.

The death of Jude

Epilogue

Boy George's gorgeous version of the title song seduces the audience into staying through *The Crying Game*'s final credits. Towards the very end of these is an acknowledgment to the Scala cinema, which now sits empty, like a decaying cathedral among the detritus of King's Cross. The once vibrant neon sign is dead and white, but still uncannily visible against the blackened exterior of this grand old picture palace. People often believe that cinemas are haunted, but the eerie sounds and movements are usually caused by the temperature drop after a full house leaves the auditorium or by the vast amounts of static electricity generated through the projectors. The Scala was not haunted, but sitting in the dark, empty auditorium out of hours it was as if the spirit of the

cinema was present, reverberating with all the different people and pictures that had passed through it.

As the film prints were taken away and the doors locked for the last time in June 1993, it seemed that the Scala's spirit also left the building. Among the thirty staff made redundant were Josh Marcroft and Tony Cooper, each of whom died later that year. The deaths of these two talented, charismatic nonconformists seem to me inextricably linked with the passing of the Scala's era; I wish it were possible to see them there again, as the miraculous ending of *Sunrise with Sea Monster* allows Donal to talk with his father one last time.

The Scala represented a chance to see movies again, and *The Crying Game* – despite the hype which implied that knowledge of the nature of the twist would spoil the audience's pleasure – is an example of a film that generously rewards second viewing. Unlike life, the beauty of film is the possibility of repeating the experience; to deny oneself that nostalgic, educative, inspirational pleasure seems unthinkable.

The Scala Cinema

Notes

1 Jack Lechner, letter to the author, 11 April 1996.

2 'Not one person in the entire motion picture field *knows* for a certainty what's going to work': William Goldman, *Adventures In The Screen Trade* (London: Warner Books, 1994), p. 39.

3 Neil Jordan, *Night in Tunisia* (London: Chatto & Windus, 1983), p. 51.

4 'The bridge that features at the start of the The Crying Game is one I knew from my childhood. For some reason I find it a convenient location for a certain type of scene, one involving characters moving from one state to the next. The same bridge featured in *Angel* and *Michael Collins*. My father died beneath that bridge, while fishing, which is why it features in my last novel, *Sunrise with Sea Monster'* (Neil Jordan, letter to the author, 16 August 1996).

In the elegant opening shot of *The Crying Game*, the camera pans along the riverbank, the distant image of a colourful fairground ominously framed by the dark silhouette of the bridge. Like the big wheel in the background, the movement of the shot is slow but inexorable, creating a sense of destiny. Drawing closer to the fairground, ambient screams are heard and the ironic title track, Percy Sledge's melancholy but pragmatic 'When a Man Loves a Woman', is deftly cut into tinny, diegetic loudspeakers.

Mona Lisa begins with a shot of Bob Hoskins crossing one of London's bridges at dawn. The opening of *Interview with the Vampire* features a lavish aerial sweep across San Francisco's Golden Gate bridge.

5 Neil Jordan, *The Past* (London: Vintage, 1993).

6 Neil Jordan, *Sunrise with Sex Monster* (London: Vintage, 1996), p. 116.

7 In *We're No Angels*, a deaf mute girl is not only saved from drowning by a statue of the Madonna but also miraculously cured. Considering both films reminds me of Jordan's description of Velasquez' *Immaculate Conception* as picturing Mary with a 'little bruised and wounded face, like a kid of about fifteen who you'd want to have sex with' (*Guardian*, 14 April 1990).

8 Jordan later said, 'I had no particular visual references for *The Crying Game*, since it was more realistic than films I had done before. All I knew was that I wanted a dispassionate style of photography. A kind of apparent realism, since the story itself took so many metaphoric turns' (letter to the author, 16 August 1996).

9 *Guardian*, 2 January 1995.

10 Frank O'Connor, *Collected Stories* (New York: Vintage, 1981), p. 6.

11 O'Connor, p. 3.

12 O'Connor, p. 9.

13 O'Connor, p. 9.

14 O'Connor, p. 12.

15 Brendan Behan, *The Complete Plays* (London: Methuen, 1990).

16 Behan, p. 237.

17 Neil Jordan, *The Crying Game* (London: Vintage, 1993), p. viii.

18 Bernard MacLaverty, *Cal* (London: Jonathan Cape, 1980).

19 Although the basic story is archetypal. For example, it could be compared to Ernst Lubitsch's 1932 drama *The Man I Killed* (aka *Broken Lullaby*), scripted by Reginald Berkeley from a play by Maurice Rostard. In Lubitsch's film a French musician drafted during WW1 kills an enemy fighter who dies in his arms. After the war the musician returns to Germany intending to confess to his victim's family but finds himself falling for the dead man's fiancée.

20 Neil Jordan, *The Dream of a Beast* (London: Vintage, 1993).

21 Stephen Woolley later said that after the night shoots of *Mona Lisa*, he and Jordan would retire to Madame Jo-Jo's for a quiet drink because in the pre-Groucho Club days this transvestite bar was one of the few places in Soho with a late licence. Woolley described Jordan as being 'astounded at how incredible the guys in the club looked', suggesting that this experience fed into the final configuration of *The Crying Game* (interview with the author, 20 June 1996).

22 *Angel* was budgeted at £450,000; *The Company Of Wolves* and *Mona Lisa* each cost £2.3 million.

23 Interview with the author, 20 June 1996.

24 *The Orange County Register*, 24 Novmber 1992.

25 Meaning the same as 'greenhouse', glasshouse is also a British slang term for a military prison.

26 CiBy had recently financed Pedro Almodóvar's camp melodrama *High Heels* (1991), but Bouygues remained oblivious of its director's sexual orientation. (See Finney, pp. 7–10).

27 Angus Finney, *The Egos Have Landed: The Rise and Fall of Palace Pictures* (London: Heinemann, 1996), p. 22.

28 According to one senior employee of Palace Pictures, the company did not develop their scripts sufficiently prior to production so that flaws remained all too present in the final films (Finney, pp. 123–4).

29 The Stockholm Syndrome is the effect whereby a hostage comes to take the side of the captors. In *The Crying Game* Jody's only chance is to make Fergus see him as a unique human being rather than a political pawn.

30 Letter to the author, 11 April 1996.

31 Interview with the author, 20 June 1996.

32 Letter to the author, 11 April 1996.

33 Finney, p. 65.

34 Frederick Elmes' credits as director of photography include *Eraserhead* (1976),

Blue Velvet (1986), *River's Edge* (1986), *Moonwalker* (1988), *Wild At Heart* (1990) and *Night On Earth* (1992).

35 Finney, p. 27.

36 Letter to the author, 11 April 1996.

37 Interview with the author, 20 June 1996.

38 Guardian Lecture, National Film Theatre, 9 May 1996.

39 Finney, p. 271.

40 Angus Finney's book *The Egos Have Landed* provides a very detailed history of the rise and fall of Palace Pictures.

41 *Irish Times*, 3 November 1992.

42 *Irish Independent*, 30 October 1992.

43 Behan, p. 204.

44 Finney, p. 123.

45 'Who's Crying Now?' (1993), a BBC 2 *Moving Pictures* special on Palace Pictures.

46 'Knight In Armor', *New Yorker*, 16 November 1992. Rafferty refers to Yeats' poem 'Fergus and the Druid' (1893), which is based on the legend of the Irish king who gave up his throne to live at peace in the woods.

47 As Jack Lechner points out, however, 'this is a trick you can only pull once, as evidenced by Miramax's lame attempt to sell the BBC film *The Hour of the Pig* in the US as *The Advocate*, with warnings not to reveal the identity – or presumably the species – of the client' (letter to the author, 11 April 1996).

48 Stephen Woolley: 'It's ironic that the editor got an Academy Award nomination because there was nothing

there to edit! So little footage was shot' (interview with the author, 20 June 1996).

49 Several players benefited from the success of *The Crying Game* in the US. Miramax's masterful release of the film preceded the Weinstein brothers' lucrative sale of their company to Disney. Following the bankruptcy of Palace Pictures, Nik Powell and Stephen Woolley were able to form a new film company, Scala Productions. The simultaneous acclaim that greeted Channel 4's E. M. Forster adaptation *Howards End* (James Ivory, 1991) and *The Crying Game* represented a sea change in the international profile of both British movies and the channel itself.

50 *What's On* (10 April 1991). In this interview given at the time of *The Miracle*, Jordan expressed interest in adapting Elmore Leonard's novel *Get Shorty*, about a loan shark who becomes a film producer, saying 'but again that would be difficult. Indeed, most things I do seem to be problematic.' *Get Shorty* was eventually directed by Barry Levinson in 1995.

51 The fourth would have been River Phoenix, who died of a drug overdose shortly before taking up his role as the interviewer. This was eventually given to Christian Slater.

52 Jordan's *Michael Collins* (1996) was first commissioned by Warner Bros. in 1984. Jordan described it as 'the best piece of writing I've ever done' (*Entertainment Weekly*, 12 February 1993), but the project became stuck in the shadow of a competing Collins biopic that was being developed by Kevin Costner.

53 The viewing figures for this broadcast were 4.125 million and 2.4 million when the film was shown again on 7 April 1996.

54 Interview with the author, 20 June 1996.

55 Jordan, *The Crying Game*, p. 8.

56 Jody: Scorpion wants to cross a river, but he can't swim. Goes to the frog, who can, and asks for a ride. Frog says, 'If I give you a ride on my back, you'll go and sting me.' Scorpion replies, 'It would not be in my interest to sting you since as I'll be on your back we both would drown.' Frog thinks about this logic for a while and accepts the deal. Takes the scorpion on his back. Braves the waters. Halfway over feels a burning spear in his side and realises the scorpion has stung him after all. And as they both sink beneath the waves the frog cries out, 'Why did you sting me, Mr Scorpion, for now we both will drown?' Scorpion replies, 'I can't help it, it's in my nature.' (*The Crying Game*, p. 16).

This fable is also told in Orson Welles' 1955 film *Mr Arkadin* (aka *Confidential Report*).

The story reminds me of James Joyce's 'old fabulist's parable' 'The Mookse and The Gripes' in *Finnegans Wake* (London: Faber and Faber, 1989, pp. 152–159). The professor tells the story of a river-bank confrontation between the Mookse (the English Pope Adrian) and the Gripes (the Irish people), the scene of which is triangulated by the onlooking Nuvoletta, the Little Cloud Girl. According to Joseph Campbell and Henry Morton Robinson's *A Skeleton Key to Finnegans Wake* (London: Faber and Faber, 1946, p. 100), 'In the fable, the hard-headed and enormously successful style of the Roman Mookse was contrasted with the more mystical, relatively quiescent and politically ineffectual style of the Celtic Gripes.'

57 Jordan, *The Crying Game*, pp. 27–8.

58 The belief is that a body double was used or that the penis is some sort of special effect (*Rolling Stone*, 1 April 1993). Yet this concept does have a precedent. Bigas Luna's 1990 film, *The Ages of Lulu* (*Las Edades de Lulú*), is 'a virtually uninterrupted succession of potent erotic imagery running the gamut of sexual variations, including sadomasochism, voyeurism, multiple sex with gays, masturbation, transvestites . . .' (*Variety*, 31 December 1990). Despite a plethora of female anatomical close-ups, the film punctiliously avoids any sight of a penis – until the central characters, Lulu and her husband Pablo, 'capture' a transvestite prostitute named Ely. Ely displays her breasts and penis, but is unable to get the attention of Lulu and Pablo, who are wrapped up in their own heterosexual lovemaking. Pablo instructs the weeping Ely to masturbate. What subtextually complicates this unedifying spectacle is that Ely is played by an actress (Maria Barranco) sporting a lifelike phallus rather than by a transvestite with silicon breasts.

59 Marjorie Garber, *Vice Versa: Bisexuality and the Eroticism of Everyday Life* (London: Hamish Hamilton, 1996), p. 231.

60 Finney, p. 274.

61 For example, in the twin sequences of Jody 'at his most defenceless'. In the fairground latrine Jody refuses to let go of Jude's hand while she seals his fate by tipping the wink to her boyfriend Fergus. Later it is Fergus who must hold Jody's hand as he relieves himself, little knowing what will be in store for him when he meets the soldier's wife.

62 Due to prolonged wrangling over the pubic hair problem, Japan was one of the last territories to open *The Crying Game*, just after the Academy Awards in 1993. Michiyo Yoshizaki explained that the Japanese critics were euphoric about the film, but it fared only moderately at the art-house market box-office, failing to cross over into the mainstream.

63 When Fergus returns to the Metro after Dil's revelation, the film does not shine a bright light in the faces of its denizens but is more sympathetic in showing how he realises it to be a gay and transvestite bar. Jordan is being 'kind to his characters' (as *The Miracle*'s Rose says a writer must be). Similarly, the scene which is unexpectedly underplayed is that in which Jude discovers Dil to be a man. Rather than milking this moment, Jordan allows it to be swallowed up in the confusion of the situation.

64 See Jordan, *The Crying Game*, p. 44.

65 Roland Barthes, *S/Z* (New York: Hill and Wang, 1974), p. 252.

66 Jordan, *The Crying Game*, p. 61.

67 Jordan, *The Crying Game*, p. 31.

68 Interview with the author, 20 June 1996.

69 Jordan, *The Crying Game*, p. 40.

70 Compare Jody's imitation of a harsh, Belfast accent ('Go back to your banana tree, nigger') to Dil's imitation of Fergus' accent, which she says is 'like treacle'.

71 *Eat The Rich* also features Miranda Richardson as a vampish bureaucrat and the Irish singer Shane McGowan as a freedom fighter demanding the return of his country.

72 *Girl/Boy* is also notable for an extraordinary sequence in which Laurie and Jo assist a man who goes into labour on a train (the 'man' turns out to be a butch lesbian travelling with her femme wife).

73 When David Henry Hwang's play *M Butterfly* (1988) was staged in London and New York, the actor playing Song Liling was identified through his initials only (BD Wong; GG Goei). At the turn of the century London's music hall audiences were captivated by a Swedish performer billed as '?Lind?' who specialised in Spanish dances. The androgynous name of this glamorous female impersonator was bracketed by question marks at a time when most drag acts were dames (blokes in frocks).

74 Jordan, *The Crying Game*, p. 67.

Credits

THE CRYING GAME

United Kingdom
1992

Production Companies
Palace (Soldier's Wife)
Ltd/Nippon Film
Development & Finance Inc
A Palace Stephen Woolley
production of A Palace and
Channel Four Films
presentation in association
with Eurotrustees and
Nippon Film Development
and Finance Inc (N.D.F.) and
with the participation of
British Screen
A Neil Jordan Film
Executive Producer
Nik Powell
Producer
Stephen Woolley
Co-producer
Elizabeth Karlsen
Associate Producer
Paul Cowan
Production Co-ordinators
Fran Triefus
Irish Unit:
Fiona Traynor
Production Manager
Irish Unit:
Gemma Fallon
Location Managers
Terry Blyther
Re-shoot:
Gilly Case
Irish Unit:
Martin O'Malley
Post-production
Supervisor
Amand Posey
Location Assistant
Scott Rowlatt
Fairground Supervisor
Irish Unit:
Bernard McCormack

Producer's Assistants
Polly Withers, Polly Leys
Mr. Woolley's Assistant
Peter Ogunsalu
Production Runner
Andrew Zein
Floor Runner
Samantha Plaisted
Post-production Runner
Sally Hodges
Production Accountant
Pat Isherwood
Assistant Accountant
Sarah Lucraft
Post-production
Accountant
Michael Garland
Casting Director
Susie Figgis
Casting Assistant
Liora Reich
Script Supervisor
Diana Dill
Director
Neil Jordan
First Assistant Director
Redmond Morris
Second Assistant
Directors
Melvin Lind
Irish Unit:
Seamus Collins
Third Assistant Directors
Jonathan Karlsen
Irish Unit:
Robert Quinn
Director's Assistant
Brenda Rawn
Screenplay
Neil Jordan
Director of Photography/
Camera Operator
Ian Wilson
Focus Puller
Kenny Byrne
Clapper Loader
Brendan Glavin

Camera Trainee
Dan Zeff
Camera Grip
Gary Hutchings
Gaffer
Norman Smith
Best Boy
Dave Escoffrey
Electricians
Ricky Pattenden,
Gary Colkett, Paul Wood
Irish Unit:
Louis Conroy, Noel Cullen,
Terry Mulligan
Rigging Gaffer
Vincent Clarke
Electrician's Driver
Martin Redrup
Editor
Kant Pan
Assistant Editor
Martyn Robinson
Second Assistant Editor
Victoria Boydell
Production Designer
Jim Clay
Art Director
Chris Seagers
Assistant Art Director
Paul Ghirardani
Set Decorator
Martin Childs
Art Department Runner
Jane Henwood
Production Buyer
Celia Bobak
Prop Master
Micky Bacon
Chargehand Standby Prop
Eddie Francis
Standby Prop
Paul Bradburn
Dressing Prop/Storeman
Rodney Pincott
Dressing Prop
Brian Aldridge
Irish Unit:
Peter Gallagher

Construction Managers
Dave Allen
Irish Unit:
John Lamon
Standby Carpenter
Tommy Westbrook
Carpenter
Irish Unit:
Brian Bassett
Standby Painter
Ken Hawkey
Painter
Irish Unit:
Bobby Scott
Standby Rigger
Con Murphey
Standby Stagehand
Brian Mitchell
Stagehand
Irish Unit:
James O'Meara
Special Effects Supervisor
Peter Hutchinson
Prosthetics
Daniel Parker
Costume Designer
Sandy Powell
Wardrobe Supervisors
Paul Minter, Clare Spragge
Wardrobe Assistant
Irish Unit:
Wendy Asher
Chief Make-up Artist
Morag Ross
Assistant to Make-up Artist
Miri Ben Shlom
Chief Hairdresser
Gerry Jones
Titles
The Optical Partnership
Music/Music Conductor/ Orchestrations
Anne Dudley
Music Perfomed by
The Pro Arte Orchestra of London
Orchestra Contractor
Colin Sheen
Music Recording Mixer
Roger Dudley

Songs
"When a Man Loves a Woman" by Cameron Lewis, Arthur Wright, performed by Percy Sledge; "Baby Jump" by Ray Dorset, performed by Mungo Jerry; "Live for Today" by/performed by Cicero, produced by Pet Shop Boys; "Second Coming" by/performed by Simon Boswell; The Crying Game" by Geoff Stephens, performed by Kate Robbins, produced by Anne Dudley; "I Only Want to Be With You" by Mike Hawker, Ivor Raymonde, performed by Kate Robbins; "The White Cliffs of Dover" by Nat Burton, Walter Kent, performed by The Blue Jays; "The Crying Game" by Geoff Stephens, performed by Dave Berry; "Let the Music Play" by Chris Barbarosa, Ed Chisolm, performed by Carol Thompson, produced by Pet Shop Boys; "Stand by Your Man" by Tammy Wynette, Billy Sherrill, performed by Lyle Lovett; "The Crying Game" by Geoff Stephens, performed by Boy George, produced by Pet Shop Boys
Sound Recordist
Colin Nicolson
Supervising Sound Editor
Eddy Joseph
Dialogue Editor
Rick Dunford
Assistant Sound Editor
Leonard Green
Footsteps Editor
Victor Nunes
Re-recording Mixer
Robin O'Donoghue
Assistant Re-recording Mixer
Dominic Lester

Boom Operator
Tony Cook
Sound Trainee
Damiano Vukotic
Caterers
Vince Jordan, Paul Duncan, Mark Camps
Unit Drivers
Terry English, Gerry Floyd
Runner/Drivers
Sara Desmond, Cheryl Willcocks
Unit Nurses
Millstream Nursing
Irish Unit:
Eileen Conroy
Publicity
Phil Symes, Michelle Sewell, Rogers & Cowan PSA
Stills
Tom Hilton
Legal Adviser
Angela Morrison
Stunt Co-ordinator
Clive Curtis
Stunt Drivers
Del Baker, Wayne Michaels, Valentino Musetti
Stunt Doubles
Helen Caudwell, Abbi Collins, Elaine Ford
Stand-ins
Steve Morphew, Marilyn Took
Special Thanks to
Frederick Elmes

Forest Whitaker
Jody
Miranda Richardson
Jude
Stephen Rea
Fergus
Adrian Dunbar
Maguire
Breffni McKenna
Tinker
Joe Savino
Eddie
Birdie Sweeney
Tommy
Jaye Davidson
Dil
Andrée Bernard
Jane
Jim Broadbent
Col
Ralph Brown
Dave
Tony Slattery
Deveroux
Jack Carr
Franknum
Josephine White
Shar Campbell
bar perfomers
Brian Coleman
judge
Ray De-Haan
David Crionelly
security men

112 minutes
10,043 feet

Dolby stereo
In colour
Metrocolor
Panavision

Bibliography

Baker, Roger, *Drag* (London: Cassell, 1994).

Barthes, Roland, *S/Z* (New York: Hill and Wang, 1974).

Behan, Brendan, *The Complete Plays* (London: Methuen, 1990).

Campbell, Joseph and Henry Morton Robinson, *A Skeleton Key to Finnegans Wake* (London: Faber and Faber, 1946).

Finney, Angus, *The Egos Have Landed: The Rise and Fall of Palace Pictures* (London: Heinemann, 1996).

Garber, Marjorie, *Vice Versa: Bisexuality and the Eroticism of Everyday Life* (London: Hamish Hamilton, 1996).

Goldman, William, *Adventures in the Screen Trade* (London: Warner Books, 1994)

Jordan, Neil, *Night in Tunisia* (London: Writers' and Readers' Publishing Co-op, 1976; London: Chatto & Windus, 1983).

Jordan, Neil, *The Past* (London: Jonathan Cape, 1980; London: Vintage, 1993).

Jordan, Neil, *The Dream of a Beast* (London: Hogarth, 1983; London: Vintage, 1993).

Jordan, Neil, *The Crying Game* (London: Vintage, 1993).

Jordan, Neil, *Sunrise with Sea Monster* (London: Chatto & Windus, 1995; London: Vintage, 1996).

Joyce, James, *Finnegans Wake* (London: Faber and Faber, 1989).

MacLaverty, Bernard, *Cal* (London: Jonathan Cape, 1983).

O'Connor, Frank, *Collected Stories* (New York: Vintage, 1981).

BFI Modern Classics is an exciting new series which combines careful research with high quality writing about contemporary cinema. Authors write on a film of their choice, making the case for its elevation to the status of classic. The series will grow into an influential and authoritative commentary on all that is best in the cinema of our time.

If you would like to receive further information about future **BFI Modern Classics** or about other books on film, media and popular culture from BFI Publishing, please fill in your name and address and return this card to the BFI*.

No stamp needed if posted in the UK, Channel Islands, or Isle of Man.

NAME

ADDRESS

POSTCODE

* North America: Please return your card to:
Indiana University Press, Attn: LPB, 601 N Morton Street,
Bloomington, IN 47401-3797

BFI Publishing
21 Stephen Street
FREEPOST 7
LONDON W1E 4AN